BUSH COUNTRY

Also by John Podhoretz

Hell of a Ride: Backstage at the White House Follies 1989–1993

A Passion for Truth: The Selected Writings of Eric Breindel (editor)

BUSH
COUNTRY

How Dubya Became
a Great President
While Driving Liberals Insane

JOHN PODHORETZ

ST. MARTIN'S PRESS ❧ NEW YORK

For Ayala

Her ways are ways of pleasantness,
and all her paths are peace.

—Proverbs 3:17

Contents

All rising to a great place is by winding stair.

Francis Bacon

BUSH COUNTRY

1

Energy in the Executive

One might conclude, from his conduct over the past three years, that George W. Bush was put on this earth to do two things:

First, to lead the United States into the third millennium, with all its terrifying challenges and wondrous opportunities.

And second, to drive liberals insane.

He's succeeding brilliantly at both.

In thirty-six months, George W. Bush has led this nation's military into two wars—innovative engagements that will serve as the blueprint for martial conflict for the foreseeable future. In those wars, he ousted two of the world's most barbaric regimes. He has committed the nation to a decades-long confrontation with the perpetrators and funders of international terrorism. He has redirected and reconceived American foreign policy to confront the threat of rogue states possessing weapons of mass destruction. He has sought to extend the democratic freedoms enjoyed by Americans to the Muslim world. He has initiated a thoroughgoing reconstruction of the structures of both the American military and the executive branch of the government of the United States.

He has forced two massive and controversial tax cuts through a sometimes recalcitrant Congress. Having campaigned for the presidency calling himself a "reformer with results," once in office Bush signed a campaign-finance reform bill and has fought for a measure that would change the way elderly Americans get their health care and pay for prescription drugs. He has imposed a new doctrine of accountability on the American education system. He has committed himself and 15 billion taxpayer dollars to the eradication of AIDS in Africa. He has been forced to wrestle with matters of the most profound philosophical significance in the matter of stem-cell research—and devised a Solomonic solution that frustrated absolutists on both sides of the philosophical divide but that fit the ambiguities of the present moment.

This would be an astonishing list of accomplishments for a president who had served all eight years in office. Bush has done it all in just three.

The best description of Bush's approach to the presidency can be found in a document more than two hundred years old—Federalist Paper Number 70. Its author, Alexander Hamilton, argues that "Energy in the Executive is a leading character in the definition of good government." Hamilton asserts that even in this self-governing nation, the president must act. He must do things, and do them decisively, creatively, and consistently. Energy in the executive, Federalist 70 continues, "is essential to the protection of the community against foreign attacks; it is not less essential to the steady administration of the laws; to the protection of property against those irregular and high-handed combinations which sometimes interrupt the ordinary course of justice; to the security of liberty against the enterprises and assaults of Ambition, of faction, and of anarchy."

The "energy in the executive" that characterizes Bush's presidency has been directed primarily toward "the protection of the community against foreign attacks." In his speech to a joint session of Congress on September 20, 2001, Bush promised the American people nothing less than his own blood, sweat, toil, and tears to defeat the foe that had attacked the country on September 11, 2001.

"I will not yield; I will not rest; I will not relent in waging this struggle for freedom and security for the American people," he said.

And he meant it.

Never yielding, never resting, and never relenting, Bush would not pursue the Al-Qaeda terror network by indicting its members and attempting to arrest them, as his predecessor, Bill Clinton, chose to do when terrorists first struck the World Trade Center in 1993. Bush believed he had to dig up Al-Qaeda by its roots. To that end, he would declare that the enemy was not only Al-Qaeda itself but the states that support and shield it—and he would commit the American military to oust Al-Qaeda's primary sponsor, the regime run by the Taliban, from Afghanistan, to achieve his goals.

At the same time, Bush was compelled to contemplate the direction terrorism might take in the future. This time the weapon of choice had been the airplane. What might it be next time? The nation got a hint when five people died and eighteen were infected as a result of mysterious envelopes laced with powdered anthrax. Anthrax was one of the substances that had come to be known collectively as "weapons of mass destruction"—a term that covered the waterfront from biological agents like anthrax to chemical agents like sarin to nuclear bombs.

The need to prevent the use of a weapon of mass destruction by a terrorist group widened the scope of the war on terror. Bush came to focus on so-called rogue states that had aggressively sought and made such weapons and seemed as though they would be nearly without constraint when it might come to passing them along.

He determined it would not be sufficient to fight Al-Qaeda. America had to confront the rogue states as well. And that led directly to Iraq. It was the only one of these countries that had consciously and consistently defied its own legal obligation under the terms that ended the 1991 Persian Gulf War to end any and all efforts to create such weapons. The natural terrorist hunger to acquire WMDs, and Saddam Hussein's desire to humiliate the United States, combined to make Iraq a new kind of threat to America and to the world.

The new threat required nothing less than a new doctrine, a subject Bush began to explore in a speech at West Point in June 2002. "Deterrence—the promise of massive retaliation against nations—means nothing against shadowy terrorist networks with no nation or citizens to defend," the president said. "Containment is not possible when unbalanced dictators with weapons of mass destruction can deliver those weapons on missiles or secretly provide them to terrorist allies. . . . If we wait for threats to fully materialize, we will have waited too long."

The war Bush waged against the regime of Saddam Hussein beginning in March 2003 was therefore an integral part of his war on terrorism. That is why Bush called it "the battle of Iraq" in his May 2003 speech announcing the end of major combat operations there. It is why Bush went before the nation on September 7, 2003, and declared that the ongoing effort to pacify Iraq had become "the central front" of the war on terror.

Bush's capacity to think about the most horrific threats and act decisively to prevent them from happening are both marks of the high seriousness with which he takes his constitutional responsibilities. They also speak to another "energy in the executive" quality that did not appear to be a hallmark of his character before he assumed the presidency: his daring.

As a presidential candidate, Bush had been quite cautious, staking out his positions on a few important matters, hammering them home again and again, never trying to get too far out in front on any issue.

He has conducted his presidency in a radically different manner. Bush will begin a public discussion by taking a breathtakingly ambitious posture—one far more ambitious than anybody, friend or foe, expected him to take. The most notable example of this was his announcement that we would make no distinction between the terrorists who attacked us on September 11 "and those who harbor them." This immediately broadened and widened the war in a way that it is impossible to believe his predecessor would have done had Clinton been in office on 9/11. With those five words, Bush changed the nature of the worldwide discussion of terrorism forever.

He has been as bold in pursuing certain domestic-policy matters. Twice he has presented Congress with tax-cut packages vastly larger than Congress anticipated. He did not attempt to make the package politically palatable to his adversaries before introducing it. He said, in effect, *This is what I think the economy needs. Take it or leave it.* In the end, in both cases, Bush did compromise, but not before the Hobson's choice he had placed before the House and Senate forced the fence-sitters to jump off the fence and grudgingly follow him.

The "energy in the executive" Bush displays in advancing his own policy is creative, tactical, and strategic. He uses it to move his agenda forward. That's the creative part. By constantly being on the move, he forces his opponents into a reactive, defensive stance. That's the tactical part. And the discussion usually takes place on Bush's terms and in a frame of reference Bush has chosen for it. That's the strategic part.

His presidential style is almost completely the reverse of Clinton's. The forty-second president of the United States was daring in the way he pursued his personal hungers. But whenever Clinton tried to be bold in matters of policy—such as the mammoth health-care plan designed by his wife, Hillary—the results were usually disastrous. The cautious, careful, even timid Clinton was the victorious Clinton. He closely followed public-opinion polls and tailored his policies to suit the public mood.

By contrast, George W. Bush has remarkable self-discipline in his personal life. To a man, his close aides describe him as the most disciplined person they've ever known. When it comes to matters of policy, however, Bush has the instincts of a successful riverboat gambler. Not the kind of gambler who is so addicted to the thrill of the easy win that he inevitably loses everything, but rather the poker player who wins most of the time by exerting the kind of self-control that a compulsive gambler cannot.

The successful poker player chooses the hands he plays. Over the course of a long game, he will make it clear to other players that he's not a bluffer. He plays when he has the cards, and they had best understand this if they don't want to lose their shirts. But as the game progresses, he quietly and deliberately uses the authority he has established. Only after he has won for real, and stayed away from losing hands, does he begin to venture into the rarefied territory that separates the truly great poker players from others: the successful bluff.

Bush showed his stuff in 2002 when it came to standing firm against Iraq. He played both the United States Congress and the United Nations Security Council with the skill of the Cincinnati Kid.

In the case of the United States Congress, the administration let it be known that its lawyers believed the president could initiate military action against Iraq without a congressional war authorization. That idea caused a firestorm in Washington, as Democrat after Democrat screamed in outrage. How could the president possibly consider going to war with Iraq absent a congressional resolution? They sputtered and hollered and fumed, whereupon the administration said: *Fine. You insist on a congressional war resolution? We'll take it.* They had little choice but to give it to him.

The gambler president found himself in a similar but far more difficult game with the United Nations Security Council. In September 2002, he laid out the case before the United Nations for forcibly disarming Iraq. His speech before the General Assembly posed a stark choice to the world body: "Will the United Nations serve the purpose of its founding, or will it be irrelevant?" The president got his way in part when the Security Council passed Resolution 1441 in November 2002, which declared Iraq in "material breach" of United Nations resolutions and warned Iraq of "serious consequences" if it continued to defy them. "Serious consequences" was a euphemism for war.

Then came five months of diplomatic sabotage on the part of France, Germany, and Russia. These three nations had voted in favor of 1441, and yet they were intent on undermining the resolution and the United States. They refused to allow a second resolution explicitly authorizing war to make it through the Security Council. Bush would have to go to war without a second resolution, relying only on the language of 1441 and the record of sixteen United Nations resolutions violated by Saddam Hussein.

His opponents at the United Nations wanted to see whether the president was bluffing. He certainly had been bluffing Congress when he suggested he might go to war without its approval. But he wasn't bluffing the United Nations. He would not allow the behavior of France, Germany, and Russia to stymie him. He stood at the head of a thirty-three-nation coalition that supported the war, and he was not intimidated by the opinion of the so-called international community or tortured by the thought of "going it alone."

Finally, Bush has shown "energy in the executive" in the realm of rhetoric. Nothing about the Bush presidency has been more surprising than the brilliance, power, and intellectual seriousness of his speeches. Bush is intimately involved in the crafting of his speeches, just as Bill Clinton was. He just hasn't felt the need to let it be known how seriously he takes the task.

As a presidential candidate, Bush became famous (or notorious) for a condition some have dubbed "dysverbia"—his peculiar tendency to add unnecessary syllables to multisyllabic words. The demands and requirements of the presidency, and his own comfort in the job, have undeniably cured him of this bizarre condition. Bush has emerged as a genuinely great speaker. He has delivered at least half a dozen speeches that rank among the most powerful and important presidential addresses of the modern era.

In a series of awe-inspiring remarks over ten days that followed a disappointingly tentative first effort on the terrible evening of September 11, 2001, Bush knit America together in its grief, celebrated its determination, and concentrated its resolve. September 11 demanded nothing less, and Bush met and exceeded the challenge. In the months and years that have followed, he has expanded on the vision he displayed during those days in a series of speeches that have created a substantive framework for a new and complex foreign policy.

And despite the know-nothing caviling of those who say that the president is overly programmed and never says anything off the cuff, Bush often speaks from notes and not from a full text. That's especially true when he's traveling around, trying to make the case for legislation on matters as various as homeland security, tax policy, and Medicare. Bush prefers to speak extemporaneously in these situations, proof of his hard-won confidence in his ability to frame the discussion.

It pains me, a former speechwriter for Ronald Reagan, to say this, but I believe Bush is the best presidential speaker since Franklin Delano Roosevelt. It pains me even more to acknowledge that I was once one of those all-too-clever journalists who believed Candidate Bush was lighter than a feather, the least-prepared person to occupy the Oval Office in the modern era. He proved me wrong. George W. Bush will face the American people as a candidate for reelection in 2004 having constructed one of the most consequential presidencies in the nation's history.

★

Now, according to those who, unlike me, maintain an unfavorable opinion of George W. Bush, he's done much, much more than that—all of it bad. His opponents and enemies accuse Bush of an endless series of crimes that began before he was president, when, in their view, he "stole" the 2000 election from Al Gore.

Moreover, according to their indictment, things have only gotten worse since his arrival in the White House. Bush, they say, has actively sought the degradation of the environment: "George W. Bush and his oil bidness pals [think] that the planet is for pillaging," in the words of Mary McGrory of the *Washington Post*.[1] He has, they charge, staged an assault on American civil liberties: "We will give to the next generation a country that none of us will recognize," according to Democratic presidential candidate Carol Moseley Braun, "a country in which librarians are forced to turn you in for taking the wrong books out of the library, in which your e-mails and your phones can be tapped, in which you can be secretly arrested and held without charges, in which you're not entitled to counsel when you have a trial. This is not the America that my ancestors fought and died for."[2]

His goal is to bankrupt the U.S. government with his tax cuts, which will simultaneously destroy the social safety net and make it impossible for future liberal presidents to institute new social programs. "There is no longer any doubt," writes Paul Krugman in the *New York Times*, "that the man who ran as a moderate in the 2000 election is actually a radical who wants to undo much of the Great Society and the New Deal."[3]

He is isolating the United States from the rest of the world, supplanting international law and multilateral organizations in favor of a go-it-alone American arrogance. "The administration has placed the United States literally above the law and in so doing has endangered us all,"[4] write Jules Lobel of the University of Pittsburgh and Michael Ratner, president of the Center for Constitutional Rights.

He is a crazed Texas cowboy, "a toxic by-product of the hierarchical plantation society of the American South," according to Michael Lind, senior fellow at the New America Foundation. Lind calls Bush's Texas "a cruel caste society in which the white, brown and black majority labor for inadequate rewards while a cultivated but callous oligarchy of rich white families and their hirelings in the professions dominate the economy."[5]

He is a cynical liar who knowingly used false intelligence to trick Americans into supporting an unnecessary war: "We know now, and perhaps the White House knew then, that the [United Nations weapons] inspectors would eventually come up empty-handed . . . so lies substituted for facts that didn't exist," writes Robert Scheer in the *Los Angeles Times,* who claims that there "exists the firm basis for bringing a charge of impeachment against the president who employed lies to lead us into war."[6]

The Bush-bashers have grown ever more alarmist over time, their rhetoric ever more purple, and their opinion of him ever more contradictory. Harold Meyerson, a columnist for the *Washington Post,* summed it all up in a cover article that appeared in the *American Prospect*: "He is incomparably more dangerous than Reagan or any other president in this nation's history."[7]

Some of these criticisms, to be sure, grow out of standard partisan frustrations. They represent the thinking of Democrats who are unhappy that a Republican sits in the White House. Such people throw around arguments, accusations, and analyses to see if any of them will stick with the American people. Though much of what they say is unfair, that they should do so is all perfectly normal and rational. Welcome to Politics 101.

But something besides mere partisan rancor is at work here. Bush's enemies aren't merely seeking advantage against him. They have come to believe in the truth and substance of their criticisms.

They actually think, for instance, that this remarkably straight-forward and straight-talking world leader—who pretty much does what he says he's going to do—is, in truth, a pathological liar. They are convinced that this follower of a mild branch of main-stream Protestant belief is a religious fanatic. They are certain that the president who has presided over an enormous increase in do-mestic government spending is actually out to destroy social-welfare programs.

And though, in fact, Bush has been obsessively concerned with the security and safety of American Muslims in the wake of the September 11 attacks, they do genuinely seem to believe that the president has been targeting ordinary Muslims for unprecedented civil liberties abuse.

The allegations grow still wilder. Bush is accused of going to war in the Middle East to benefit the tiny state of Israel, serving Jewish interests rather than the interests of peace. Some of those who hurl this accusation have simultaneously compared him to Adolf Hitler—an opinion that might, one would think, appear inconsistent with the notion that he is a servant of the world's only Jewish state.

The likening of Bush to Hitler isn't merely a product of the imaginations of scruffy protestors demonstrating in city streets. Such literary celebrities as Gore Vidal and Norman Mailer have offered coy suggestions that they agree with this sort of thing. Vidal calls the present government "the Cheney-Bush junta," while Mailer describes the Iraq war as a kind of last gasp for a would-be master race on its way out, a quick-and-easy cure "for the ongoing malaise of the white American male."[8] Nor is the Bush = Hitler idea confined to the world of leftist, America-hating American intellectuals. Germany's minister of justice,

Herta Daeubler-Gmelin, made the analogy in a preelection talk in September 2002.[9]

★

The conservative demon of left-liberal fantasy may wear a Bush mask, but the real George W. Bush is a far more complicated figure ideologically, especially on certain hot-button conservative issues. Though gun owners are enthusiastic Bush supporters, he has continued to defy the wishes of the National Rifle Association by supporting a ban on assault rifles. On affirmative action, to take another instance, he personally directed his Justice Department *not* to argue for eliminating the use of race as a positive factor in college admissions when it made its arguments in two connected 2003 Supreme Court cases involving the University of Michigan. (The Bush administration opposed only assigning a specific numerical value to minority status.)

Bush has issued some of the most eloquent and moving anti-abortion rhetoric of any Republican. And yet he has made decisions on related issues that have made it clear he is in no way in the pocket of the pro-life movement. Pro-lifers wanted Bush to ban all research into stem cells because they fear research will inevitably lead to the harvesting of human fetuses for the extraction of such cells. His answer to the problem was to permit continued stem-cell research on those stem cells that had already been isolated for research—but to forbid further harvesting of fetal stem cells pending further review.

His enemies, typically, have tended to characterize the stem-cell decision as a giveaway to anti-abortion fanatics. But what Bush did was something quite extraordinary. He found a middle ground on one of the most morally convoluted questions of our day. His decision did not drag those who consider stem-cell research a horrifying evil into an impossible position. Nor did it end all stem-cell research. Bush managed to take an unorthodox position on this most difficult of moral questions without igniting a culture war.

Indeed, the key to understanding Bush's stands on a number of domestic political issues is that he wants to call a truce in the culture war that has divided the people of the United States for thirty years or more. Perhaps because he has a real war to fight, or because he is temperamentally unsuited to the role of culture warrior, Bush is searching for all kinds of new ways to address divisive social concerns.

This is risky territory for a Republican politician, because the base of the Republican Party is partly built on the culture war— on fighting liberals when there are showdowns over racial and gender preferences, sexual license, and ways to handle matters such as crime. Risky or not, however, it is Bush's natural territory. The real, as opposed to the opposition's fictional caricature of, George W. Bush has advanced certain liberal interests and causes—particularly in the realms of education, campaign finance, and a prescription-drug benefit. In a less politically frenzied world, honest and sensible liberals and leftists might acknowledge the fact.

But alas for them, the real George W. Bush is invisible to his adversaries. Their inability or unwillingness to see him as anything other than the villain they fear, or wish him to be, offers a new wrinkle in what the liberal historian Richard Hofstadter called "the paranoid style in American politics."

Bush's successes are literally driving them crazy.

Taken together, all of Bush's presidential qualities mark him as a genuine leader and a transformative figure on the American and world stages. Love him or hate him, respect him or revile him, George W. Bush has made extraordinary use of the powers of the presidency and has changed the United States, its government, and the world in ways that have made an indelible mark on the new century.

We are now living in Bush Country.

Crazy Liberal Idea #1

Bush Is a Moron

One of the primary characteristics of Bush Country, according to Bush's critics, is that he isn't up to the intellectual demands of the presidency. Or, to put it more bluntly, that he's a moron.

This opinion has long offered perverse comfort to Bush's opponents. Paul Begala, the Clinton campaign consultant, put it most succinctly on a cable television program in June 2000. Revising the slogan he and James Carville devised for Bill Clinton in 1992, Begala said: "It seems to me it's still 'the economy' but 'Bush is stupid.' "[1] Begala later wrote a book titled *'Is Our Children Learning?': The Case Against Prezident George W. Bush.*[2]

The basis for the charge is, of course, the way Bush consistently mangled the English language during the 2000 campaign. The leftist Web site Politex counted a list of twenty-eight words he had mispronounced or misspoken. Jacob Weisberg, the editor of *Slate.com*, has produced two slim volumes of "George W. Bushisms" full of solecisms. Gail Sheehy, the journalist who has spent a lifetime practicing psychology without a license, pronounced Bush "dyslexic" in a *Vanity Fair* article. This led Bush to utter an inadvertently hilarious retort: "The woman alleged that I had— said I had dyslexia. I never interviewed her."[3]

Reporters who traveled with him for months on his presidential campaign had taken to calling Dubya "the English patient."[4] In October 2000, the leftist intellectual Todd Gitlin put it more ominously in an article titled "It's the Stupidity, Stupid": "Follow W.'s gaffes more carefully and something more sinister than sloppiness emerges. . . . Bush gives ample evidence that he does not reason. He thinks not in logical arcs but in scatters. There's a slapdash disorder to many of his infelicities—they are piles of disconnected words, a sequence of flash cards."[5] All this helped give rise to the dominant caricature of Bush—the fun-lovin', brainless himbo played by Will Ferrell on *Saturday Night Live* with a perpetual smirk on his face and a beer in his hand, uttering invented words like "strategery."

The trope was not retired with Bush's ascension to the presidency. In June 2002, Joan Smith, a columnist for the *Independent,* a British newspaper, wrote: "It is hard to imagine any world leader being afflicted with quite the degree of bovine incomprehension that the President habitually displays."[6] In July 2003, Senator Bob Graham, then seeking the Democratic nomination for president, staged a scene in a bookstore for a *Washington Post* reporter, knowing full well that the reporter would write it up: "Bob Graham balanced the book in his left hand and considered it. . . . He read the title aloud: *Team Bush: Leadership Lessons from the Bush White House.* 'Hmm,' he deadpanned. 'Must be a short book, must have large print.' . . . He flipped open his cell phone and called an aide. 'I've got something for you,' he said, repeating the title. Then he started to laugh. 'No,' Graham said. 'It doesn't come with cray-ons.' "[7] As a candidate trolling for support among the Democratic Party faithful, Graham believed his emergence as a Bush-is-stupid basher might score him some desperately needed points.

Feel-good sites for Bush-haters proliferate across the Web, with names like Presidentmoron.com, Bushisamoron.com, and Toostupidtobepresident.com. The manifesto of the latter states: "Surely, there have been smug, duplicitous, rich whelps who have served as President of the United States. But, [sic] none of them have [sic] been quite as dumb as George W. Bush."[8]

The hunger to believe in Bush's idiocy has led many on the left-liberal side of the ledger into embarrassing missteps. One Bush critic, Joan Walsh of *Salon.com*, was dismayed to learn that the seventeen-year-old Dubya's combined SAT score had been exactly the same as hers (1200, back when the SAT was actually difficult).[9] "In July 2001," reports Byron York, "a fictional 'study' purporting to show that George W. Bush had the lowest IQ of any recent president spread across the Internet. . . . The fictional researchers determined that Bush's IQ was 91—precisely half that of Bill Clinton's 182, which was said to be the highest of recent presidents. The hoax should have been easy to spot. . . . Never-theless, the IQ story struck some of the president's critics as so believable that a few of them, including newspapers in Britain and Europe and *Doonesbury* cartoonist Garry Trudeau, reported it as fact."[10]

Despite having made a fool of himself by falling for the IQ hoax, Trudeau was unembarrassed later to write of Bush that "it never occurs to him that it might be important for the Leader of the Free World to express himself with clarity and coherence."[11] (Evidently, Trudeau is an expert on the matter because of his wide experience writing clear and coherent words that can fit into balloons that float over the heads of cartoon-strip characters.) Trudeau's sentence appeared in the introduction to the second volume of *George W. Bushisms,* which was published in 2002— many months after Bush put to rest any doubts among any but the most tin-eared that he was more than capable of presidential statesmanship.

★

In the wake of Bush's post–September 11 performance, the Washington writer Andrew Ferguson observed that "the paradox of George W. Bush continues to puzzle the enlightened classes. The paradox is simply this: How could the inarticulate bumbler of the 2000 campaign—a fellow so intellectually undistinguished, so clearly 'not one of us'—prove to be such a deft and powerful leader?"[12]

What disturbs Bush's critics most is that he does not act in accord with the reigning cultural affect of the American chattering classes (among whom I include myself). We pride ourselves on self-aware displays of cleverness, constant references to popular culture and the latest trends, and a hunger for sharing the trivia we know with others. To be sure, knowledge of popular culture is not enough—it's also important to drop the names of the novels we're reading and make it clear we remain conversant with the works of philosophy and history through which we ploughed in high school and college. We are drenched in irony. We don't like to take anything too seriously.

This affect is what connotes intelligence to those who consider themselves the most intelligent people in America. It was very much the affect of Bill Clinton—indeed, he may have typified the style.

This is not Bush's affect, to put it mildly. Ferguson used *New York Times* reporter Frank Bruni's well-reported book on the Bush presidential campaign, *Ambling Into History,* to explore "the paradox of George W. Bush." Ferguson pointed out that while Bruni tries very hard to be fair to Bush, "the disdain is never far from the surface. . . . Bruni dutifully cites instances of what he calls, with exquisite condescension, Bush's 'moderately active mind.' Bush read and liked a detective novel Bruni recommended, for example—evidence of excellent taste, clearly."

Still, Bush's knowledge base is unacceptably spotty, in Bruni's view: "When someone mentioned the word 'vegan' one day, Bush looked confused. He didn't know what that was. . . . When somebody suggested he was a bit of a 'yenta,' he flashed befuddlement. He didn't know what that was, either. . . . [Bush] had apparently never picked up a *People* magazine and never surfed the channels and rode the wave of *Access Hollywood* or *Entertainment Tonight.*"[13]

It is actually offensive to the chattering classes that the president is not conversant with the kind of cultural trivia that fill our brains. It is somehow a strike against him in this group's eyes that Bush dares to be unaware of those who feed themselves within a particular substratum of vegetarianism; that he isn't up on garment-center Yiddishisms; and that he should confuse Roger (*007*) Moore with Michael (*Stupid White Men*) Moore.

Ferguson concludes:

> The Bush paradox rests on a misapprehension—one shared
> by American journalists and intellectuals from Tom Paine

through Henry Adams and H. L. Mencken, right on up to, well, Frank Bruni and much of today's Washington press corps. Gazing down on their subject from Olympian heights, reporters wonder why the gifts of the intellectual—for language and rumination and subtlety—aren't indispensable to the exercise of power. And indeed they aren't. Leadership requires will, self-confidence, and moral clarity. These Bush has in abundance. And the best bet is that he will continue to demonstrate them, day by day, even as his intellectual superiors puzzle over their self-made paradox.

In the first volume of *George W. Bushisms,* editor Weisberg quotes scornfully from a Bush appearance on CNN in September 2000: "There is book smart and that kind of smart that helps do calculus. But smart is also instinct and judgment and common sense. Smart comes in all kinds of different ways."[14]

Why Weisberg would have included this remark in his catalogue of gaffes and bloopers is far from clear. What Bush said is patently true, and applies not only to himself but to many extraordinarily intelligent people. You have to begin from the premise that Bush is an idiot to find this self-description ludicrous.

A straightforward reading would suggest that Candidate Bush understood himself very well—or, perhaps, that he understood the great political value of not acting as though one is the smartest person in the room.

In any case, Bush's supposed lack of literacy is belied by Bruni's own account. Bush may not make a show of his sensibility, but he is a reader—occasionally of serious fiction. Bush not only read the detective novel Bruni recommended, but also loaned the *Times* reporter his own copy of Tim O'Brien's literary novel about politics, *In the Lake of the Woods.* Lewis Libby, who works as Vice President Richard Cheney's chief of staff, is himself the author of a fine work of literary fiction called *The Apprentice,* about a seventeen-year-old Japanese boy who gets mixed up in a complex conspiracy in a bathhouse in the year 1903. The president read *The Apprentice* closely. Bush is also a devotee of books by and about Winston Churchill. Bruni tells how Bush was once terrifically annoyed when it was suggested that he had claimed an interest in the great British prime minister and historian in an effort to gull the cable chat-show host and Churchill enthusiast Chris Matthews. "Do you think," Bush asked Matthews, "that I'd take time out of my life to research what the hell you like?"[15]

Okay, say some Bush-loathers. Maybe he's not a *blithering* idiot. But he has no clear-cut intellectual interests, and took only three trips outside the United States before beginning his run for the presidency, and therefore might as well be considered one. "Bush is plenty smart," according to Garry Trudeau, "and he's technically educated, but because of his lifetime incuriosity about the wider world, Bush has fought a crippling, life-long battle with ignorance."[16]

Jonathan Chait of the *New Republic* was appalled to discover in the early months of 2001 that "the prevailing image of Bush has flipped, from dumb moderate to wily conservative. But why couldn't Bush be both conservative and dumb?" By "dumb," Chait said he meant "not a lack of innate intelligence but a persistent incuriosity that has kept him in a state of childlike ignorance."[17]

The story that especially sickened Chait had to do with Bush's inquiries about the treatment of the American crew of a spy plane shot down by China in April 2001. The president wanted to know how the health of the detainees was, whether they had

Bibles, and whether they were being allowed any exercise. Chait dismissed these queries, which actually seem rather relevant to the subject of how to interact with China on the matter of that country's handling of Americans being held captive there, as "the sorts of questions a second grader would ask." Not any second grader I've ever met.

Chait's contempt in part has to do with the fact that the president asked about exercise, for another favorite liberal gimmick is to accuse Bush of being more interested in working out than in policy. Note this immortal passage by Maureen Dowd of the *New York Times*: "The more buff the president grew, the more [Republican] party solons worried that he was frittering away time in the gym that could be better used formulating clear policies. . . . He looks too good. . . . [Vice President Dick Cheney] can't get off the ticket because Mr. Bush won't get off the treadmill."[18]

In fact, those closest to Bush say that his extraordinary physical condition has allowed him to maintain a dazzling degree of focus and concentration on the details of the war on terror and the war in Iraq. One member of the Bush family said that he thought George Bush the Elder was the hardest-working man he'd ever seen until he had a chance to observe the way in which Dubya approached his duties. (To be sure, this testimony from Bush associates and relatives will be rejected out of hand by the Bush-haters, who will assume that it is merely spin.)

The best that some on the Left can find to say of Bush is that he should not be easily dismissed, no matter how stupid he may seem. In the words of Mark Crispin Miller, author of *The Bush Dyslexicon,* "Although Bush is indeed illiterate, bone-ignorant and generally illogical, he's not a cretin. At the nastier kind of politics, he is extraordinarily shrewd. In this he is a lot like Richard Nixon,

who, as I argue, is his spiritual father. Bush only benefits from
his wide comic reputation as a genial idiot (he's neither genial
nor an idiot). We 'misunderestimate' him at our peril."[19]

Miller is referring to Bush's most famous "Bushism." In Ben-
tonville, Arkansas, on November 6, 2000, Bush told a cheering
crowd: "They misunderestimated me." The term has stuck not
because it makes Bush look foolish but because it captures something about the nature of Bush's opposition—and the opposition
to Republican leaders for the past fifty years.

The notion that Republican leaders are often "amiable
dunces"[20] has been a persistent feature of liberal Democratic
thought since the election of Dwight David Eisenhower in 1952.
Eisenhower's ideological and partisan opponents consistently portrayed him as an inarticulate and doddering incompetent. Think
of it—the great man who did nothing less than manage the European theater in World War II, and later served as president of
Columbia University, was deemed intellectually wanting by the
chattering classes of his day!

Ronald Reagan came in for the same treatment—Reagan, a
voracious autodidact who wrote his own newspaper columns, radio commentaries, and innumerable speeches as he traveled the
country working for General Electric for more than a decade.

Only poor Dan Quayle came close to resembling the caricature—and yet even Quayle, the much-ridiculed misspeller of "po-
tato," had won a surprise victory for the United States Senate at
the age of twenty-nine and had become an important player there
on such matters as national defense and job retraining.

Now there's George W. Bush, who doesn't know whether
Friends is a TV show or a movie and says Christ is his favorite
philosopher, rather than Plato or Jean-Paul Sartre. The "amiable

dunce" cliché maddens conservatives as much as it pleases liberals. But perhaps conservatives should stop grousing and start smiling over it. The consistent inability of Democrats and liberals to pay proper respect to their adversaries has surely done more damage to them than to those they disrespect.

Their misunderestimation will continue to cost them as long as they persist in their comforting delusion that the whip-smart George W. Bush is an idiot. After all, Bush has described himself as "the master of low expectations."[21] So, basically, he's come right out and said it: People who think he's a sucker are being played for suckers.

2

Voyage 'Round His Father

Only two sets of fathers and sons have served as president. It took 161 years for the country to try a second time after its experience with John Quincy Adams, the son who lasted a single sad term from 1825 to 1829. There have been a few other cases of consanguinity. Two Harrisons have lived in the White House: the unfortunate William Henry, who caught pneumonia on the way to his inauguration in 1841 and died a month later, and his grandson Benjamin, who led the country into a massive depression between 1889 and 1893 and was booted out. Only the Roosevelts, distant cousins, were both successful presidents sharing a surname.

This is surprising. Talent runs in families, so it would stand to reason that a talent for politics runs in families as well. Moreover, politics is somewhat demystified for the children of politicians. For most of us, political leadership, and the means whereby support is gained and votes are won, poses a mysterious and insuperably daunting challenge. For one thing, it requires a great deal of public speaking, and poll data tell us that more people fear public speaking than they fear death. But if your father goes out every few days and stands in front of an overcooked piece of chicken smiling at the folks and saying the same thing he said three years before and two years before and last year and last week, public speaking might not seem fearful any longer. It will be just an ordinary working task, like writing a memo is to a midlevel executive.

So, too, with fund-raising. How on earth does one person ask another for cash money for his own personal use? There are only two types of people who do this as a matter of course: beggars and politicians. The sense of shame that keeps most of us from standing on a street corner and shaking a tin cup would keep most of us from getting on the phone and doing what pols call "dialing for dollars." Such a chore is infinitely easier for those who have seen it done since childhood.

Thus it is that, over the past two centuries, in towns and counties, there have been scores upon scores of would-be dynasties. The Kennedys are the most famous, of course; the Rockefellers ran several states at once; and there have been Gores and Byrds, Longs and Livingstons. But none of those would-be dynasts made it to the top.[1]

Most tellingly, none of this nation's greatest political leaders ever produced a scion with great political abilities. Who were the sons of Thomas Jefferson? Andrew Jackson? Abraham Lincoln? Teddy Roosevelt? Woodrow Wilson? Their biographers know, and so do the historical societies and libraries dedicated to their lives and lore. But most of us have no idea, and that is precisely the point.

Great men do not often father great offspring. Plato presumably had children. We know Shakespeare did. We know Rousseau abandoned his. We know Tolstoy had dozens, mostly by his wife. Those children have vanished into the mists of obscurity. Great men blaze paths of glory. But those paths scorch the earth they have walked on and leave their sons to walk on the smoking coals they have left behind.

We might come up with all sorts of pat pop-psychological explanations for the relative lack of filial greatness. The parental shadow was too vast for them ever to emerge from it. The father was too involved with his own life mission to help mold and sculpt his own children. The children spend their lives as students and disciples of their fathers and can never find their own way.

But the mystery deepens when one notes that the same phenomenon holds true for the not-quite-great and their offspring. Some great men, it is true, are the children of prominent but not immortal parents. Anthony Trollope's mother was a bestselling writer. The pessimistic philosopher Schopenhauer once taunted his own mother, a noted writer of her day, with the prophetic and appropriately grim accusation that history would remember her only as Schopenhauer's mother.

What of undistinguished presidents and their children? This situation might seem like the best of all possible worlds. The sons get all the knowledge anyone could need about power and fame, but don't have to wrestle with a legacy of true greatness. Well, it might seem like the best of all possible worlds, but it turns out it isn't. Only one such son of an undistinguished president has risen: George W. Bush.

So let me propose, from this brief history of presidential paternity, that it's no easier to be the son of a failed president than it was to be the son of a great president. Maybe it's more difficult, in fact. Men who fail are consumed with self-justification, and that's surely even more true for those who failed on a grand scale—like a failed president. The justifications and excuses are always the same: They did poorly because they were treated unjustly, or because they were the victims of a conspiracy, or because they were just too good, too pure, too noble, to succeed in an imperfect world.

Such justifications tend to consume not only the justifiers but also their family members, who feel obliged to offer the kind of loyalty to the paterfamilias that his party, his voters, and his nation did not. Watching someone you love and worship go through the public death of a massive political defeat may well be so agonizing that their children would never willingly risk it for themselves. So, whether his father is a giant or a pygmy, no matter: It's nearly impossible for the son of a president to become president.

Nevertheless, for those who detest George W. Bush, his standing as a "First Son" (to purloin the title of Bill Minutaglio's superb biography) constitutes a central charge in the indictment against him. One of the nation's foremost leftist journalists summed up the indictment in an e-mail to me: "It's the whole privilege thing: Non-achieving, smart-ass, goof-off drunk rich kid gets into National Guard with Daddy's help, shirks it while he's in there, gets set up in oil biz through Dad, fails, gets set up in baseball 'cause of Dad and rich benefactors who owe his dad, manages to turn $700,000 into $14 million . . . just gets gets gets throughout his life, and then to top it off gets the effin' presidency even though he didn't really win."

This is quite a bill of particulars. I could argue that he didn't shirk his National Guard service, that he didn't get particularly rich in the oil business, that he turned the Texas Rangers into an enormously profitable baseball team and profited fairly as a result, and that he won the presidency fair and square. Still, the journalist's indictment carries with it a kernel of the truth about George W. Bush. The very fact that Bush made it to the presidency while carrying this kind of baggage—baggage that makes him entirely fair game for this sort of attack—reveals why he is such a singular figure in American political history.

★

Americans tend to like politicians who come from modest circumstances. Ronald Reagan was the son of the town drunk of Dixon, Illinois. Bill Clinton's father was a traveling salesman who was hit by a train while the future president was still in his mother's womb. Richard Nixon was born to a struggling Quaker family. Jimmy Carter grew up on a farm. Harry Truman didn't go to college. And on it goes, backward and upward, to the greatest of Americans: Abe Lincoln, resident of history's most legendary log cabin.

Coming from a wealthy and powerful family presents a problem for rich-boy politicians. The good fortune of their birth to well-heeled parents can be bad fortune when it comes to national politics. They may have every material advantage, but how can they find common ground with poor people, with struggling lower-middle-class people, with anybody except the privileged? They have usually solved the problem by emphasizing details from their personal histories that suggest they haven't actually had it all that easy. John F. Kennedy's campaign leaned heavily on his wartime heroism. Franklin D. Roosevelt, it was known, had nearly been killed by polio. Even the Rockefellers, sons of the richest man in America, had their own hard-luck story: To teach them the value of money, their father gave them a mere dime's allowance a week.

When the time came for George Bush the Elder to introduce himself to the American people in 1988 after eight years as vice president, he certainly didn't talk about his upbringing as the grandson of a founder of a Wall Street investment bank and the son of a United States senator. Instead, in the convention acceptance speech drafted for him by Peggy Noonan, Bush began his life story with his heroic naval record in World War II, skipped over his years as a Big Man on Campus at Yale University, then picked it back up with his move to Texas in 1948: "Those were exciting days. We lived in a little shotgun house, one room for the three of us. Worked in the oil business, and then started my own."

This was a pretty decent simulacrum of a classic American success story. Even though Bush the Elder grew up dressing for dinner in a household with a butler, a chauffeur, and manservants, he still managed to offer himself up as a go-for-broke entrepreneur with that can-do American frontiersman spirit.

George W. Bush couldn't come up with a story that pleasant when he ran for president twelve years later. In truth, he didn't have much of a story at all. In three years between college and graduate school, Dubya had three jobs, worked on three different political campaigns and considered running for the Texas state legislature. He served in the Texas National Guard.[2] He had girlfriends. He graduated from business school and got married. He ran for Congress once and lost. He drank and quit. He smoked and quit. He did various things in the oil industry but didn't hit it big. He became the public face of the Texas Rangers baseball team with a small ownership stake. Then, in 1994, he ran for governor of Texas and won—and six years later was president of the United States.

Dubya had the most meteoric rise in American political history. To some degree, certainly, he has his father and his upbringing to thank for it. But what his critics fail to see is that any advantage he might have had in 1994 and 2000 was equaled by the disadvantage of being George H. W. Bush's son. For one thing, his father's tattered reputation among core Republican voters throughout the 1990s was a liability for Dubya, even in Texas. Bush the Elder lost the 1992 election in part because he alienated Republicans by raising taxes and advancing the most ambitious and costly big-government legislation since Richard Nixon's first term (the Clean Water Act, the Americans with Disabilities Act). The very sound of the name "Bush" provoked anger among many politically active Republicans. Among less political Republican voters, the Bush name inspired little but yawns. Some of them voted for Bush the Elder for reasons of entropy in 1992; others stayed home; and at least 5 million of them evaded party lines by voting for the independent candidate, H. Ross Perot. Thus, the fact that he shared the name and bloodline of a recent president gave Dubya incomparable name recognition, but it wasn't necessarily the name recognition he would have wanted.

After he was elected in Texas—in a come-from-behind victory in which he crushed a popular sitting governor—Dubya was still suspect in the eyes of many Republicans because of his patrimony. When he advocated a complex tax-reform system in Texas to help shore up school funding in less affluent areas of the state, some

Republican activists were horrified, because it seemed to them that a tax-reform plan devised by a Bush must have had a tax increase hidden somewhere inside. In the two years leading up to his presidential run, Dubya was forced to spend an enormous amount of time and effort convincing party bigwigs and intellectuals that—ideologically speaking—he bore little relation to his father.

And his lack of a touching, pull-yourself-up-by-your-bootstraps American success story cost Dubya plenty at the voting booth in 2000, both during the Republican primaries and the general election. When it came to presenting himself as a role model for the American people, Dubya seemed to have little to offer other than that he was a loving husband and a good Christian who had put bad habits aside to live a godly life.

During the primaries, for example, Dubya was wildly outmatched in the personal-history department by John McCain, the man with perhaps the most dramatic and heroic life story in contemporary American politics. The courage and endurance McCain had shown in his years as a prisoner of war was enough to rally millions to his side for that reason alone. McCain's self-sacrifice seemed especially powerful and moving by contrast with the spiritually slovenly and morally compromised Bill Clinton. Republicans understood that their best shot in 2000 was running as the anti-Clinton party. Bush rode that theme hard by promising to inaugurate a "responsibility era." But McCain was the far more convincing anti-Clinton, and Bush had to surmount McCain's advantage.

Surmount it he did, by defeating the war hero in the primaries before meeting his closer biographical match in Al Gore in the general election. If Dubya had been able to tell a bootstraps story about himself, it would surely have been an immeasurable help

VOYAGE 'ROUND HIS FATHER   35

against Gore—for Gore's life story was oddly similar to his. The sitting vice president was a preppie Ivy Leaguer who was raised in a residential hotel in Washington, DC, disconnected from ordinary American realities. He attended Sidwell Friends, the quintessential Washington private school, around the same time that Dubya was attending Andover, the quintessential New England boarding school. Like Dubya, Gore had a distinguished father casting a long shadow over him. Albert Gore Sr. served seven terms in the House of Representatives and three terms in the U.S. Senate, exactly the same posts his son would later hold. Albert Gore Jr. had literally been bred, so his very own father said, to be president.

Gore was haunted daily by his father's example. He said as much in interviews. He talked about having studied *The Drama of the Gifted Child,* an earnest little book by Swiss psychoanalyst Alice Miller that became all the rage around the time people began referring to themselves not as adults but rather as "adult children." The drama of the gifted child, according to Miller, is that gifted children are usually raised to fulfill the ambitions and expectations of narcissistic parents. Gore Jr., who was already in his sixth decade when he was running for president, was openly grappling with the challenge of being the political son of a prominent political father trying to make it to the presidency. He was not only trying to be president. Al Gore wanted to be the first Adult Child President.

Dubya has no patience for this kind of thing. In one of the few personal attacks he launched during the 2000 campaign, Dubya referred slightingly to the fact that feminist Naomi Wolf, a Gore consultant, had told Gore that he needed to be an alpha male and wear clothing in earth tones to prove it. Bush brushed aside most inquiries about the unique psychological position he found himself in. His reticence on these matters is a distinct family trait. "Don't put me on the couch. There's nothing there," Bush the Elder once said. The son often used the same sort of language.

Yet George W. Bush has lived "the drama of the gifted child" every bit as much as Al Gore. His family called him "Little George." He found out he was being sent away from his Texas home to the same Massachusetts boarding school his father had attended on the very day the acceptance letter from Andover came in the mail. And Little George returned home from school, and later from college, to take up summer chores and jobs and tasks that were either secured for him or assigned to him by his father. In short, in every outward respect, he was to the manor born. Something, however, kept Little George apart. He could easily have joined the Eastern Establishment during his years at Andover and Yale. He could have remained East, made his fortune on Wall Street, could have lost his Texas accent and lived the life of a preppie. He had been born in New Haven while his father was finishing his college years at Yale. He had spent weeks every summer with his two sets of Connecticut grandparents. He had been dressing for dinner from a very young age. He knew what to do with a finger bowl. As part of his "drama of the gifted child," Little George made the conscious choice to be a Texan through and through.

And therein hangs a fascinating tale. Bush and his family say that one of the defining moments of his life was when experience taught him there was something terribly wrong with the mindset of liberal elite opinion. That moment came in 1964, on the campus of Yale University. The freshman Bush, then eighteen years old, was walking across the quad when he spied William Sloane Coffin, the school's rock-star-famous chaplain. Dubya had just returned from Texas, where he had witnessed the painful defeat of Bush the Elder in his first political race for the U.S. Senate. He introduced himself to Coffin, who had been at Yale with Big George.

"Oh yes, I know your father," Coffin said. "Frankly, he was beaten by a better man."

The cruelty of Coffin's remark is hard to take in all at once. Here was a respected elder figure at Yale speaking to an eighteen-year-old kid. The elder offers a spontaneous and unprovoked attack on the kid's dad. The boy naturally has no capacity to respond. He isn't the elder's peer. And yet he is made to suffer an attack on his father's honor; an attack, moreover, issued with a casual hauteur. "You talk about a shattering blow," his mother told the *Washington Post* thirty-five years later. "Not only to George, but shattering to us."[3]

In 1998, Coffin wrote George W. to ask his forgiveness for a remark he did not remember making. "I believe my recollection is correct," the future president wrote back. "But, I also know time passes, and I bear no ill will."[4]

The Coffin incident helped put the collegiate George W. Bush at odds with the Eastern Establishment he could easily have joined without a look back. If Coffin was the best the East had to offer, then Dubya would be what he had been as a child—a Texan.

★

"My dad was shy," Dubya told the *Chicago Tribune* in 1992. "I never had any sense of what his ambitions were for me."[5] The son may not have known what his father intended for him, but he certainly knew what his father wanted for himself—the presidency. Dubya's friends have attributed his decision to quit drinking altogether on his fortieth birthday in 1986, his most impressive act of will, to a fear that he might do something that reflected badly on his father when Big George began his run for the presidency. According to Joe O'Neill, who was with Dubya that day, "He looked in the mirror and said, 'Someday I might embarrass my father. It might get my dad in trouble.' And boy, that was it. That's how high a priority it was. And he never took another drink."[6]

These stories—and the fact that he led a fairly undistinguished life until after his fortieth birthday—have led many to compare George W. Bush to Shakespeare's Prince Hal, the slumming ruffian nobleman who transforms himself into the great nationalist king Henry V upon his father Henry Bolingbroke's death. Prince Hal has been a grave disappointment to his father, who fears that his son will never achieve the gravitas necessary to be a good king. "Riot and dishonor stain the brow of my young Harry," Henry IV says.

After September 11, noted Chris Matthews, "the country discovered it had a young leader rising to the occasion, an easygoing Prince Hal transformed by instinct and circumstance into a warrior King Henry."[7] On CNN, Jeff Greenfield volunteered that "it's a little bit like, you know, Prince Hal becoming Henry V."[8] Veteran Washington presidential adviser David Gergen: "When trouble hit, how rapidly we left behind the pages of *Henry IV* and suddenly we seem to be into the pages of *Henry V*. There had been a transformation as young George W. Bush stepped up."[9]

This seems at first like an apt analogy, made all the more so by Dubya's acknowledged history as a problem drinker. But it's far too facile. For one thing, Prince Hal does genuinely, seriously, bad things. He's a thief, a pickpocket, and a whoremonger. George W. Bush drank a lot and played a lot of pool volleyball at the apartment complex in Houston where he lived before getting married in 1977—nothing so bad. For another, Prince Hal was helped along in his debauchery by a father figure named Falstaff, who gave him the love and attention he couldn't get from his disapproving father. George W. Bush has no father figure but his own father.

Most important, Prince Hal consciously chooses to be a scapegrace because he thinks it will help him in future years:

> *By so much shall I falsify men's hopes;*
> *And like bright metal on a sullen ground,*
> *My reformation, glittering o'er my fault,*
> *Shall show more goodly and attract more eyes*
> *Than that which hath no foil to set it off.*
> *I'll so offend, to make offence a skill;*
> *Redeeming time when men think least I will.*

In other words, Hal is saying, *I'm behaving badly now because it will make me appear better later.* That was not George W. Bush's story. There was no real rebellion in him. For most of his life, he was the best of sons, to such a degree that he surely did himself some damage.

He worshipped his father, and sought to follow Bush the Elder's path. He had struggled to get into Yale because it was his father's alma mater. He wanted to play baseball like his father, who had been a high school and college star, but wasn't quite good enough. He sought entry into the Texas Air National Guard, according to one official of the guard, because, he said, he wanted to learn to fly "just like his daddy," who had been a World War II flying ace.

He became affianced at the age of twenty, just as his father had been (though the engagement ended when Dubya's intended dumped him for another man). He made his first run for public office seeking a seat in the U.S. House of Representatives in 1978, just as his father had sought a House seat in 1964—and, again like his father, lost it amid accusations that he was a rich-boy Easterner.

Bush the Elder's Connecticut background had proven a huge liability in his first try for office in Texas. His rival in his 1964 House race, Ralph Yarbrough, scored points against Big George by portraying him as a "carpetbagger," a Northeastern liberal in Texas Republican clothing. In 1978, Little George's opponent played exactly the same Texas-hold-'em card. Kent Hance accused Dubya of being "an outsider as far as understanding our problems." In a debate, he turned to Bush and mentioned that a farmer in his district had seen a limousine with "one of them Connecticut licenses. That where you from, George?" Dubya joked that he had been born in Connecticut only because his mother had been there at the time and he hadn't been given much of a choice. But he couldn't overcome Hance's insinuation.

Dubya could not establish an independent identity. For a long time, he did not try to. He went into the oil business, like his old man had. He raised money from members of his family for various efforts at oil exploration and exploitation. Then, in 1986, Dubya sold his company in Texas and moved to Washington—

not to advance his own career but to help get his father elected
president. He was forty years old. And he was moving closer to
his father—both figuratively and geographically—rather than further away. As he entered his fifth decade, Dubya was Little George
more than ever, it seemed.

★

The Bush family is exceptionally tight-knit. And demanding. Loyalty is expected, encouraged, and rewarded. It became Little
George's role in the 1988 campaign to extend the demands of
loyalty beyond the family to everybody who came to work for
the Bush campaign and the Republican Party as a whole. He was
a campaign emissary to the Republican Party's Christian-
conservative wing. It was his job to assure Christian conservatives,
who were less than faithful to his father's brand of old-style Re-
publicanism, that if they gave his father their support, his father
would reciprocate by hewing to their views on social issues like
abortion. "You'll be astounded at how conservatively he'll govern,"
Little George told conservative chieftain Paul Weyrich.[10]

George W. Bush's place in his father's shadow appeared to be
a permanent residence, and one he relished and took comfort in.
Everybody on the campaign referred to him as "Junior," even
though he wasn't a junior (and only campaign manager Lee At-
water dared use the word to his face). After his father's victory
in November 1988, Dubya became part of a hush-hush group
called the "Scrub Team," working to vet every single potential
candidate for employment in the new Bush administration to
ensure that there were no disloyal elements. Moreover, two years
into his father's presidency, it was Junior who flew to Washington

from Texas to let his father's White House Chief of Staff, John Sununu, know that Sununu had lost the confidence of the president and needed to find another line of work.

Dubya was close to power, but the power wasn't his. And despite his oft-expressed loathing of "psychobabble," he was quite aware of the problematic position he found himself in. He talked about it openly in 1988, during the Republican convention that nominated his father. "I want to make it clear," Dubya told the *Houston Chronicle,* "that I'm not running for anything right now, but if I do decide to in the future, I'd have to work hard at establishing my own identity."[11]

Every son has to work hard in that way, of course—whether he's the son of a prominent politician or the son of the town drunk, like Ronald Reagan. On the surface, of course, it may seem like the town drunk's son has a far more difficult row to hoe, because his paternal example is one of disappointment and weakness. Transcending such a forebear is extraordinarily difficult, because it is an act of betrayal. It requires acknowledging the failure of the beloved father and using him as a negative role model. The failure-father is what you don't want to be, what you must design your life to avoid becoming. This act of paternal abnegation is nearly impossible for most men, and their inability to achieve it helps account for multigenerational poverty and domestic abuse.

But consider the challenge posed to the son of a prominent man, like George W. Bush. He may want nothing more than to be like his father. And yet he cannot really make his own way in life without emerging from the parental shadow. So how can he emerge from that shadow when it's such an alluring, comfortable, and safe place to be?

What made it possible for George W. Bush to move forward as a politician and a man was his father's defeat in 1992.

★

By all accounts, Little George was devastated and made furious by Big George's pounding at the hands of Bill Clinton and Ross Perot. And yet he was also let loose.

In 1988, Bush had mused about his father that "it would probably help me out more if he lost. He'd be out of politics and a private citizen."[12] Dubya certainly didn't mean to say anything revelatory and deep. He meant that the son of a sitting president would have difficulty running for office because everybody would simply think he was riding his father's coattails.

Even so, it was a revealing remark. In 1998, his wife Laura described her father-in-law's defeat as nothing less than a liberation, both for him and his brother Jeb: "In many ways, the '92 defeat, as hard as it was on George and Jebbie—in a lot of ways it was the first time in their lives they were liberated from the shadow of their Dad. It was literally the first time they felt like they could say whatever they thought, without it reflecting on their father."[13]

Both sons ran for governor in 1994. Jeb lost in Florida (he would win four years later). Dubya won in Texas. Now, you could leave it there. You could say the older generation was forced into retirement and the younger generation moved up, simple as that. That's what Dubya said in 1994: "For the first time in our family, Dad knew he was not going to be the center of attention. It was another generation's time."[14]

It wasn't anywhere near that simple. Bush the Elder, for instance, made it clear that he expected his younger son Jeb to win in Florida—but he had no such confidence about his namesake's chances in Texas. That was partly a reflection of political reality. Dubya seemed to be facing a much tougher race than Jeb. Still, the world knew then (and knows now) that George the Elder basically expected George the Younger to lose his big race.

George Bush the Elder is a very discreet man. The fact that his doubts were made so public suggests (a) perhaps little more than yet another example of his lack of political vision, or (b) a lack of faith in his own son, or (c) some serious parental competitiveness.

The 1992 defeat of Bush the Elder has brought out competitive qualities in both Georges. They have said some notable things about each other over the past ten years—things that are not especially kind. Dubya in 1994: "For the first time in our family, Dad knew he was not going to be the center of attention."[15] Former president George H. W. Bush on his son's gubernatorial victories: "I'm amazed, I'm still amazed, at how he's done."[16] President George W. Bush, April 25, 2003: "I really don't spend a lot of time hashing over policy with him. He knows that I am much better informed than he could possibly be."[17]

These sorts of comments suggest there's a testier, pricklier relationship between father and son than anyone will ever really know. Both men publicly affirm their love for one another, of course; President Bush has said that though he doesn't discuss policy with his father, their conversations are important to him. They're "more along the line of a dad and a son, a dad conveying to his son how much he loves him. Which is important, even at the age of fifty-six years old it's important."

This a touching thing to say—maybe. Looked at another way,

however, it may not be touching at all. One might even imagine that the current president has consigned the former president to the category of emotional supporter rather than adviser, counselor, or guide. He has, in other words, taken his father and reduced him in size and grandeur. The shadow is gone. Or, to be more precise, it's George W. Bush who casts the shadow and George H. W. Bush who is now resident in it.

According to Bush family lore—the public part of that lore, at least—the only acknowledged moment of bristling family conflict between Little George and Big George came in 1973, when the twenty-seven-year-old Dubya took his fifteen-year-old brother Marvin out on a bender around Washington, DC. They arrived home to find Big George waiting, furious. "I hear you're looking for me," Little George said to Big George. "You want to go mano a mano right here?"

They didn't go mano a mano, of course. But when Little George really chose to take on his father, it came in a far more profound arena than a Washington living room on a drunken December night. It came in the arena of presidential power, where George W. Bush would advance the Republican Party out of the pinched and parsimonious spirit under which it suffered during his father's tenure and replace it with an expansive, positive, even exuberant, spirit of his own.

★

Make no mistake. The presidency of Bush 41 provided a valuable blueprint for Bush 43. That blueprint could have been called "How Not to Be President." George W. Bush has examined the blueprint with staggering attention to detail—and done everything the opposite way. It was as though he were following to the letter the advice of Francis Bacon to all those who aspire to greatness: "Neglect not also the examples of those that have carried themselves ill in the same place, not to set off thyself by taxing their memory, but to direct thyself what to avoid."[18]

George Herbert Walker Bush is one of the finest human beings ever to serve in the White House—a man of infinite personal grace and dignity, loved and admired by almost everyone who worked for and with him. But he was a disaster as a president and a party leader. He was consumed with process—with the orderly direction of government. He believed his primary job was managing the executive branch. He disdained visionary programs, visionary ideas. He wandered all over the ideological map. He did not seek to advance his ideas, or any ideas, for that matter. Two and a half years into his presidency, his chief of staff, John Sununu, announced that the administration had no more goals to achieve in domestic policy—that the Elder Bush had done all he wanted to do, which hadn't been all that much to begin with.

At some point, and we can guess that the point came in the midst of the calamitous 1992 campaign, the son came to see the totality of his father's failure clearly and mercilessly. In practical terms, Bush the Elder did not have a well-functioning White House or executive branch. In political terms, he had lost all ability to get his legislation through the Democratic-dominated Congress—and had alienated Republican members of the House and Senate at the same time. He also alienated voters in the Republican base, which led to the creation of two insurgent candidacies that helped destroy him—one led by Patrick J. Buchanan during the primary season and the other by H. Ross Perot in the general election. In economic terms, Bush the Elder had nothing to offer voters when things went sour. In public-relations terms, he was unable to do anything to staunch the flow of negative stories about him. And in the area of foreign policy, which really mattered the most to him, he was continually a step behind, as the world changed radically around him with the collapse of Communism.

In his presidential-campaign book, *A Charge to Keep,* Dubya[19] says his father's chief failing in 1992 was that he allowed his rivals to "define" his presidency. "During the 1988 campaign, my dad was able to define himself. In 1992, Bill Clinton and Ross Perot and Pat Buchanan defined him, and he lost in a long and miserable year. You die a death of a thousand cuts in politics, and his opponents inflicted them. . . . I'm convinced objective history will judge his presidency far more kindly than the 1992 election did."[20]

That's the loyal son speaking, blaming his father's enemies for their unscrupulous cleverness in "defining" the old man. The truth is far more interesting than that, and George W. Bush's own, painstakingly anodyne autobiographical book reveals just how clear the truth was and is to him.

A Charge to Keep was drafted in 1999, when Bush and his team knew they had to "define" the Younger Bush to some degree by pointing out the various ways in which he would govern the country more like a Reagan than a Bush. He used the book to make this case. In it, he explicitly renounces his father's decision to renege on his pledge at the 1988 convention—the flattest and simplest campaign promise ever made. "Read my lips," the Elder had said. "No new taxes." As the Younger notes affectlessly in *A Charge to Keep,* "Several years after he made that pledge [not to raise taxes], he and his advisors decided to forge a compromise with Congress. He traded some tax increases for spending re-straints. Dad knew it would cost him politically, but decided to do it nonetheless. . . . Breaking his pledge cost him credibility and weakened his base."[21]

The Younger Bush understood that a leader who loses credibility with the voters loses everything. Both as a candidate for governor and president, George W. made only a few very large domestic-policy promises and then hewed to them with single-minded dedication. He said he would push through an education-reform package as governor and president, and he has. He stuck to his tax-cutting plan in both Austin and Washington. He fought for a faith-based initiative in Washington, as he promised he would. He put together a commission to propose reforms for Social Security, as he vowed he would. He has pushed to open the Alaska National Wild-life Refuge for oil exploration, just as he insisted he would.

Some of his promises have been enacted into law. Others have not, and likely will never be (Social Security reform). Some of them (the education bill especially) bear little relation to the spe-cific point-by-point proposals he offered during his campaign. But still, George W. Bush has kept his promises.

One could argue that's because he believes strongly in what he has proposed. That's true of many of his proposals. But as a strictly political matter, George W. Bush has stood his ground because he came to believe that it would cost him big-time to change his tune. He learned that a president shouldn't welsh on his word, because he saw what happened when his father did.

The Elder Bush's calamitous decision on taxes had another, even more significant, effect on the Younger. Remember that the Elder Bush didn't promise to *cut* taxes in 1988. He said he would not levy *new* taxes, and couldn't even hold to that minimal

promise. George W. Bush began his run for the presidency with
the knowledge that the name "Bush" was deeply associated in
the minds of Americans with a tax increase, and it is hardly an
accident that as a presidential candidate he ran on a proposed
tax cut that by some calculations is the largest in American
history.[22]

The son's passionate advocacy of tax cuts isn't just a political
lesson well-learned. It is nothing less than a philosophical renun-
ciation of the father's political legacy. The one thing for which
Bush the Elder receives praise even today from the political establishment is the budget deal of 1990, in which he raised taxes
as a political trade-off for congressional spending limits. But instead of celebrating and paying tribute to his father's "courage,"
as so many in the liberal media have done, Dubya reached back
over his father to embrace the economic philosophy of Ronald
Reagan, who is still reviled by much of that same liberal media.

★

The Bush family has a very complicated relationship to Ronald
Reagan and his legacy. Reagan beat the Elder Bush at the polls
in 1980 before elevating him to the vice presidency. What's more,
Reagan actually campaigned against Dubya during the Younger
Bush's first run for office in 1978—and nobody in politics forgets
a blow like that. And yet here George W. Bush is, casting himself
and governing as the true heir of Ronald Reagan.

That's especially true on matters of foreign policy, where
George W. Bush's divergence from his father is even more pronounced, and, given his father's passionate interest in the subject,
even more of a betrayal. Ronald Reagan was a revolutionary when

it came to matters of foreign policy. He pursued radical new measures, like the Strategic Defense Initiative (Star Wars), which by promising protection against nuclear attack effectively overturned the three-decades-old policy of Mutual Assured Destruction that had governed U.S.-Soviet relations. He demanded the destruction of the Berlin Wall. He went to Moscow and talked about democracy. He encouraged a tide of democratic change in Latin and South America. Ronald Reagan was a universalist who believed that democracy could take root anywhere and everywhere because freedom is the essential condition of the human spirit.

George Bush the Elder had a far less sentimental, far more conventional view of foreign policy. In his view, the world was a messy place, and what mattered most was stability. He didn't much celebrate the signature world event of his presidency, the fall of the Berlin Wall. As the Soviet Union was collapsing, Bush the Elder actually tried to hold the Evil Empire together. He did the same with Yugoslavia as that tripartite state naturally decomposed. He had a thuddingly literal notion of what he called "the new world order." He was far more interested in the "order" part than in the "new" part. Even his greatest achievement, the expulsion of Iraq from Kuwait in the first Gulf War, ended up being a rigorous enforcement of the status quo. Once Saddam Hussein was out of Kuwait and things were back as they had been before, he ended the war and left a mess that bedeviled his successor, Bill Clinton, and which his son was finally compelled to try and clean up once and for all twelve years later.

George W. Bush has taken Ronald Reagan's universalist vision of democracy and advanced it by applying it to the one region in the world about which even Reagan never spoke in democratic terms. When addressing the Israeli-Palestinian conflict, he talks in

terms of a democratic Palestine—and suggests that only a democratic Palestine will be an acceptable solution to the conflict both
for him and the world. And, most remarkably, he talks about
democracy for Iraq, a notion that apparently never occurred to
his father.

★

The son's ability to see beyond the father he loves to the politician
who failed is a mark of the cool-eyed detachment that is necessary
for political greatness—the capacity to detach yourself from your
surroundings, examine reality with a cool head, and then act. You
have to act not according to the fantasy that would make your
life easier, but according to the reality that's staring you in the
face.

In 1997, two years before he began his run for the presidency
but right around the time he decided to go for it, Dubya told
NBC News: "I don't have time to worry about being George
Bush's son. Maybe it's a result of being confident. I'm not sure
how the psychoanalysts will analyze it, but I'm not worried about
it. I'm a free guy."

I'm a free guy. He is freer than most of us will ever be because
he freed himself by doing something incredibly difficult, something that no other son of an American president has been able
to do. He was able consciously to betray his own father's legacy—
and thereby become president. And he has continued to betray
his father's notions of how to conduct the presidency and what
a president's approach to world politics should be—and has
thereby become not just a better president but a great president.

Crazy Liberal Idea #2

Bush Is a Puppet

George W. Bush has constructed his presidency as an ideological rebuke to his father's—and yet to many of his critics, Dubya is a mere pawn in a dynastic effort to restore the Bush family to its rightful place atop the nation.

"W. is methodically renovating his dad's legacy," wrote Maureen Dowd in February 2001. "Keen to protect the family honor, the new president is going back, piece by piece, working to sand away the scars of Bush I. . . . If the Bush name was tarnished by leaving Saddam in power, W. can fix that. . . . If the Bush name was tarnished by breaking the no-new-taxes pledge in an honorable effort to cut the deficit, W. can fix that. He can ignore the deficit and cut taxes."[1]

So, according to Dowd, even though it might have appeared that Dubya was turning his back on his father, the son was actually working to serve his father's interests! This twisted interpretation is typical of a common slander against George W. Bush.

The notion is that George W. Bush is a tool of powerful men, powerful interest groups, and powerful ideological alliances. He is putty in their hands. He does what they tell him when they tell him, because he has no views of his own and nothing but air in the space between his ears.

The problem is that Bush's opponents can't decide just who controls him. Every time Bush does something that would suggest he makes up his own mind and makes his own decisions, some among the chattering classes decide that he has simply changed controllers. As a result, the list of Bush's controllers has grown, changed, and is full of peculiar contradictions.

From the outset of his gubernatorial campaign through his election as president, it was said that Bush was merely the marionette and his aide Karl Rove was the puppeteer. More than that: Rove was "Bush's Brain."[2] Indeed, in a horribly nasty book about Rove with that title, two Texas journalists simply declared him "co-president of the United States" and suggested that "the influence of Karl Rove on the president may raise constitutional questions."[3] Constitutional questions, yet!

Rove is undeniably influential, a real power behind the throne.[4] But it's far from clear that he's even the most influential presidential aide of our time. Surely the person who deserves that title is Henry Kissinger in his years as national security adviser. No one assumed Nixon had little to do with foreign policy because Kissinger was powerful in his own right. For his part, Rove has described Bush admiringly as "the kind of candidate and officeholder political hacks like me wait a lifetime to be associated with."[5]

In any case, soon after the administration began, many Bush opponents decided that Rove was not the puppetmaster. No, the real puppetmaster was Dick Cheney. The vice president was, we were told, a father figure for Bush (even though Cheney is only five years Bush's senior). The taciturn Cheney did not speak much to the press and would not share the nature of his discussions with his boss. Since Bush was, in the eyes of his critics, so obviously unserious, they assumed Cheney was making all the decisions.

Bush put Cheney in charge of a task force to design an energy strategy for the United States. Everybody knew what the centerpiece of the energy strategy would be—the exploration of the oil fields resting under the Alaska National Wildlife Refuge (ANWR). Everybody knew this, because Bush had discussed the matter at a level of detail uncustomary for him throughout his presidential campaign. Bush had worked in the oil industry for a decade, and was convinced of the vital importance of increased exploitation of domestic oil deposits. Though ANWR exploration was a subject near and dear to Bush's heart, his placement of Cheney at the head of the task force designed to sell the idea to the American people was taken as a sign of Cheney's control over *him*.

In the imaginings of those who believe that everybody who has ever made a nickel from searching for or selling oil is at best morally compromised and at worst evil, the Bush-Cheney team was evidence of an even more powerful and terrifying puppetmaster at work. Bush was nothing more than a shill for the oil companies, doing their bidding at the expense of America's precious natural resources. This notion assumes that no one could actually believe this country would benefit from pumping more of its own oil—both in terms of its economy and as a matter of foreign policy. Only shills for the oil companies could possibly argue such a ludicrous thing.

Well, I, for one, believe it—nor am I alone in this—and I

have never received a nickel from an oil company. As it happens, I do not assume that people who disagree with me are in the pay of foreign oil producers who would lose power if the United States were the source of more of the world's petroleum products. Rather, I assume they disagree with me out of a conviction about the pristine nature of the Alaskan environment or the dangers of fossil fuels—a conviction I recognize but do not share. It would be interesting to see whether such people could extend those with whom they disagree a comparable degree of intellectual courtesy. So far the prospect looks bleak.

When it comes to George W. Bush, his opponents know little or nothing about courtesy. "The United States Inc is currently being run by an oligarchy, conducting its affairs with a plutocratic effrontery which in comparison makes the age of the robber barons in the late 19th century seem a model of capitalist rectitude,"[6] writes the usually marvelous cultural historian Simon Schama in the *Guardian,* thereby displaying what in his case especially is a shocking ignorance both of the present political moment and of the late nineteenth century.

Nor can such opponents even see reason when their own arguments begin to crumble around them. Many of them thought, for example, that the collapse of the energy firm Enron would be a black mark against the administration. Surely the public would now understand how Enron and Bush were the same. Paul Krugman of the *New York Times,* in a remark that will go down as one of the more hilariously wrong-headed statements in the annals of punditry, went so far as to say: "I predict that in the years ahead Enron, not Sept. 11, will come to be seen as the greater turning point in U.S. society."[7]

Enron was in Houston, you see, and Bush had been governor

of Texas. Enron contributions to the Bush campaign totaled
$645,000. Bush had a fun nickname for Enron's chief executive.
One former Enron official worked as secretary of the army. But
when the administration refused to lift a finger to bail Enron out
of its troubles and instead allowed it to fail of its own accord,
the argument that Bush was a puppet of Enron failed along with
it. The anti-Bush faithful even had a ready-made answer for this
one: Bush might not have been specifically a puppet of Enron,
but Enron wasn't really an oil company anyway. It was an *energy*
company.

With the build-up to the war in Iraq, the view that Bush was
an oil-company puppet came roaring back in 2002. Why? Because, we were informed, the war in Iraq would actually be "about
oil." Remember the "no blood for oil" signs carried by antiwar
protesters across the country? In their estimation, Bush was sending hundreds of thousands of Americans into harm's way for
"oil."

But if Bush's chief interest in Iraq was gaining ready access to
its oil, he didn't have to go to war. All he needed to do was go
to the United Nations and request that the world body drop the
sanctions it had imposed on the free flow of Iraq's black gold
back in 1991. After a while, the illogic of the "war is about oil"
view became too much even for the Bush-haters.

And at that point, the search for the real Bush puppetmaster
took a new and disgusting turn.

As the president demonstrated his relentless determination to
ensure that Saddam Hussein and his totalitarian regime were
wrested from power, many of his opponents decided that he was
now under the control of an evil cabal so powerful that it could
override even the hypnotic sway of Big Oil. This cabal comprised

administration officials who were not even senior enough to be in the cabinet, which only helped to prove how brilliantly manipulative they could be. Indeed, some of the cabal's members weren't even administration officials at all—more proof of just how long and terrifyingly adroit its tentacles were.

The members of the cabal were the "neoconservatives." Its leader was said to be Deputy Secretary of Defense Paul Wolfowitz, who had worked with Bush on the campaign and was the only member of the group to have been granted a special pet name by the president ("Wolfie"). Others inside the administration supposedly included Lewis Libby, Cheney's chief of staff; Elliott Abrams of the National Security Council;[8] Douglas Feith, Dov Zackheim, and Abram Shulsky, all of whom worked for Wolfowitz at the Pentagon; and Richard Perle, who was an unpaid adviser as head of a defense-policy review board. The key characteristics of the neoconservative cabal, in the reckoning of those who assume it exists, are unconditional support for the Israeli right wing led by Prime Minister Ariel Sharon coupled with an almost orgasmic thrill at the thought of committing American troops to combat. The group's interpreters have come to this understanding because they have read articles and editorials written by certain of its members who work outside the administration, among them William Kristol and Robert Kagan of the *Weekly Standard*.

What links all these people together? It is true that they all know one another. Many of them are friends. Some attended college and graduate school together. They share a belief in a muscular American foreign policy, a belief that the use of American power to solve problems in the world will lead to greater stability and freedom. They are supporters of the state of Israel.

And they are all Jews.

In brief, many Bush opponents have taken to arguing that George W. Bush has come under the control of a collective of Jewish advisers whose true purpose is not the defense of the United States but the furtherance of Israel's security interests. Thus, at the beginning of the twenty-first century, the determination to believe that George W. Bush does not make his own decisions has given new life to a classic canard of hate.

Colin Powell and Condoleezza Rice, Bush's two principal foreign-policy advisers, are not Jewish. Nor is Dick Cheney. Nor is Donald Rumsfeld, his secretary of defense. Nor is George Tenet, the director of central intelligence. Nor is Richard Armitage, who as deputy secretary of state stands at precisely the same bureaucratic level as Wolfowitz.

And yet, in the view of Michael Lind, whatever arguments these top-level officials might make or positions they might take on matters of war and peace count for nothing by contrast to the power of the neoconservative cabal. "The neocons took advantage of Bush's ignorance and inexperience," Lind has written. "It is not clear that George W. fully understands the grand strategy that Wolfowitz and other aides are unfolding. He seems genuinely to believe that there was an imminent threat to the U.S. from Saddam Hussein's 'weapons of mass destruction,' something the leading neocons say in public but are far too intelligent to believe themselves."[9] So if the neocons did not actually believe that Saddam was a threat—which is a ludicrous assertion—what was their secret purpose in compelling Bush to go to war with Iraq? Well, to force America to serve the Jews, of course.

In my view, there is no difference—no difference whatever—between this line of argument and the portrait of Jewish power described in *The Protocols of the Elders of Zion,* the document forged by czarist secret police to justify murderous pogroms against Jewish peasants. "Claims that the purpose is not to protect the American people but to make the Middle East safe for Israel are dismissed by the neocons as vicious anti-Semitism," Lind has written. Indeed they are—as such claims are dismissed by all people of good will, and for one reason: Because they *are* vicious anti-Semitism.

In an effort to deny Bush ownership of his presidency and the policies he espouses, some Bush-haters will evidently stop at nothing. They will not even forswear the use of rhetoric that should remain beyond the pale.

3

Return to Reaganism

When he took the oath of office on January 20, 2001, it did not look as though George W. Bush would be able to change much of anything. Indeed, there was ample reason to believe he would not be able to govern at all. The new president had not won the nationwide popular vote in 2000, which made him the first chief executive to govern in such a fashion since Benjamin Harrison in 1888. Add to that the bizarre circumstances surrounding the recount of Bush's 930-vote margin of victory in the state of Florida and its final resolution by a sharply divided Supreme Court, and all the ingredients were present for governing stasis, even calamitous failure.

Tens of millions of politically engaged Americans were indicating that they simply would not accept Bush's legitimacy. They believed the Supreme Court decision was a coup by judicial fiat. The conservative Republican response—that their opponents had lost and should "get over it"—only enraged the anti-Bushites all the more. The Gore supporters weren't really sore losers. They were outraged losers. And outraged losers can make a great deal of trouble for a weakened winner.

Even though Republicans retained their majorities in the House and Senate that year, offering the incoming president some hope of getting a fair hearing for his agenda, the results of the 2000 election were full of ominous portents for them and for Bush. The combined non-Republican vote total for president (Al Gore plus the Green Party's Ralph Nader) was 53 million—3 million more than Bush received. This was a significant turn of events, because it suggested for the first time in two decades that presidential voters might actually be shifting markedly to the Left.

Gore, running a more frankly liberal campaign than the centrist Clinton did in 1992 or 1996, got almost 3 million more votes in 2000 than Clinton had in 1996—and 7 million more than Clinton had in 1992. It's beyond dispute that if Ralph Nader had not run in 2000, Al Gore would be president today. That means Gore's defeat was not due to a presidential electorate that preferred the views of George W. Bush. No, Bush prevailed because to a small but meaningful part of the Democratic electorate, *Gore* was not quite left-wing *enough*.

The Gore/Nader success at the polls was sobering news for conservative Republican triumphalists who had spent the previous twenty years believing that the majority of the American electorate was innately sensible and therefore innately Republican. Even the loss of the White House in 1992 after twelve years of Republican rule had proved this point to many conservatives (among whom I include myself), who blamed the Elder George Bush's loss on Bush's own deviation from conservative orthodoxy.

Bill Clinton's reelection in 1996 could also be interpreted in this conservative light. Though Clinton was a sitting president with a booming economy in a time of peace, he still couldn't get even 50 percent of the vote against the somnolent Bob Dole and the whacked-out Ross Perot. Clinton actually prevailed in his two elections by leaning to the Right on certain issues. In 1992, he advocated tax cuts. In 1996, he ran as the president who signed the bill abolishing the lifelong right to welfare.

In 2000, by contrast, Gore abandoned the Clinton formula of tacking rightward by taking an aggressive and explicitly populist tone. Gore did not run as Bill Clinton's heir, the way George Bush the Elder had run as Reagan's heir. His key appeal was to class resentments. Farther out on the Left, Ralph Nader offered a message about how American capitalism was running amok both here at home and across the world. And together Gore's and Nader's anti-Republican message proved more popular than the Republican one proffered by Bush.

Those 53 million non-Republican presidential votes meant that Bush became president without a clear-cut mandate. The situation was such that some conservatives even speculated in the days following the November election that Bush might be better served by not fighting to prevail in Florida. They feared that in 2001, America would not be able to tolerate a president's winning in the electoral college but not in the overall vote tally.[1]

It also seemed that Bush's ability to get a move on as president might be profoundly affected by the thirty-six-day recount period, which had stymied his team's capacity to plan for their incoming administration. The monthlong delay meant that the new administration had to take office with a skeletal political crew. The transition between the outgoing Clinton and incoming Bush administrations was hurried and incomplete. Paul Light, the universally acknowledged Inside-the-Beltway expert on executive-branch staffing, described the new administration's status in dark terms. "The continued delays do create the very real possibility that the next president will still be assembling his cabinet and making policy choices long after the 2004 presidential campaign begins," Light wrote in December 2000. "That is a morning after that may make the winning candidate wonder whether he might have been better off going down with the ship after all."[2] It did not take Bush anywhere close to that long, but it was nearly a year before he was able to fill the key jobs in all the cabinet departments and executive agencies.

Then there was the matter of the president-elect's lack of experience as an elected official, and almost total lack of personal experience when it came to playing the Washington game. Bush arrived at the White House having served only six years in elective office as governor of Texas. He hadn't even governed much in two of those six years, having spent them running hard for president. Not to mention that even when the governor of Texas is working night and day, he's still not governing much. The Lone Star State is the nation's second most populous, but its governor is a constitutionally weak public official. The Texas railroad commissioner, by some reckonings, has more power than the state's governor. Would Bush know how to handle the demands of the presidency?

Making matters even more dicey for Bush was the difference in atmosphere between Washington and Austin, Texas's capital. Bush managed things well in Austin because he was able to work closely with Democrats. He forged an uncommonly close relationship with the Democratic leader of the Texas House, Bob Bullock. (Bullock even endorsed Bush for reelection in 1998.) He said, and he clearly believed, that he could duplicate his friendship and alliance with Bullock in Washington.

Washington ain't Austin. Democrats in Texas aren't all that ideologically dissimilar from Texas Republicans, whereas in Washington, Democrats and Republicans exist as separate tribes warring hotly over desirable territory. Thanks to the electoral maps provided by the television networks on Election Night 2000, those tribes even came to have recognizable colors. Bush's states were colored red, Gore's states were colored blue. The election revealed that there was a huge cultural gulf between Red America and Blue America. A close analysis of the county-by-county results (there are 3,309 counties in the United States) told the story. The more urban the county, the more Democratic it was. The more rural, the more Republican. Democrats had vast advantages on the highly urban East and West Coasts of the United States and across the Industrial Belt in a pattern the Washington writer and editor Tod Lindberg called "the broken arc." Republicans owned the South and much of the nation's midsection. Red America and Blue America had little in common culturally or politically. Indeed, they seemed actively to dislike each other's values and core convictions.

Bush spent a great deal of time during the 2000 election trying to file the rough edges off his Red America appeal. He and his team made sure the 2000 Republican nominating convention in Philadelphia was dominated by African-Americans, Hispanics, and women. But their three-day act of sentimental political positioning couldn't really disguise the truth about Bush. Remove the packaging and there he was: A born-again, pro-gun, pro-life, pro-school-choice, tough-on-crime, anti-Hollywood, anti-gay-rights Texas guy.

The neat fracture between Red and Blue America was the best explanation of why and how relations between the political parties had grown so foul in the 1990s—and why Bush seemed ill-equipped to cope with the rottenness. The people who work in Washington politics do so out of love and loathing in equal measure. They love the stated ideals of their party and loathe what they believe to be the true purpose of the other party. Inflicting defeat on the adversary is what gives them pleasure. It also seems ennobling; the believers think they're fighting on behalf of core principles. This is as true for Republicans as it is for Democrats. Republicans went after Bill Clinton with everything they had, and Democrats were lying in wait for payback. Bush tried to short-circuit the partisan attack on him by refusing to speak directly about the moral and ethical troubles of his predecessor. "I have no stake in the bitter arguments of the past few years," he said during the 2000 campaign.

But those bitter arguments are the fuel that makes Washington run (some people say money makes Washington run, but, as usual, people who think money explains everything are wrong). Policy battles infuse politics with passion and meaning. Politicians and their lackeys pay public lip service to the idea that they all want to work together to accomplish important goals for the American people. Yet the last thing they want to do is work together, and everyone in Washington knows it. With rare exceptions, mostly in the realm of foreign and trade policy, the party that does not hold the presidency will do everything it can within reason—and sometimes in a way that surpasseth reason—to thwart the president.

So there was George W. Bush on the cold morning of January 20, 2001—damaged goods, inexperienced, with a country that

seemed on an ideological journey away from him. Bush did have
that majority to help him in Congress, but it was razor thin—
and it would be gone in the Senate in four months' time anyway
when liberal Republican Jim Jeffords decided to declare himself
an independent and vote with the Democrats.

This was the political reality facing Bush as he began his presidency. And yet it transpired that he was not fatally compromised,
or injured, or wounded. How did he overcome?

★

Bush pulled it off by doing exactly what an unimaginative political adviser would have told him not to do: He set up camp on
the Right. An unimaginative political adviser would have looked
at the realities of the situation and told Bush to move to the
political center. He should sue for peace, try to make the best of
a bad situation. This was the advice offered him by self-appointed
wise men like David Gergen, the Super-Elastic-Man of Washington politics who can work for any president, arguing any position,
because he himself believes in nothing. Bush did make a few
token gestures toward bipartisanship. He appointed a Democratic
congressman, Norm Mineta, as secretary of transportation, and
the superstar academic John DiIulio, a conservative Democrat, as
the head of his effort to design and implement "faith-based"
social-service initiatives. But that was about it. Bush chose to line
up with the ideologues in his party rather than the dealmakers.
Indeed, in many of the cases where he did otherwise, Bush lived
to regret it—especially in his choice of treasury secretary. He
allowed himself to be talked into appointing former Alcoa CEO
Paul O'Neill for Treasury, largely because O'Neill was a close

friend of Fed chairman Alan Greenspan and therefore might be able to influence the man who controlled interest rates and the money supply. O'Neill was nothing short of a disaster; he spent a year redesigning the offices at his department, caused international financial ripples with incautious remarks about monetary policy, and kept confidently predicting bright prospects a few days before the economy would take another turn southward.

Bush had reason to be far more content with the choices he made based on ideological commonality. For his attorney general, he made the surprise appointment of John Ashcroft, recently defeated in his effort to win reelection for the Senate in Missouri. It would be fair to say that Ashcroft was a breathtaking selection. A minister's son who anointed himself with oil after he was elected governor of Missouri, Ashcroft was a favorite son of the Religious Right. Ashcroft was instantly attacked on the spurious grounds that he had no business being attorney general of the United States—when Ashcroft had once been the attorney general of the state of Missouri, not to mention that state's senator and governor. By any rational set of criteria, he was among the most qualified men ever to serve as attorney general. What his critics really meant was that they didn't like Ashcroft because he was too religious for them. They were just too mealymouthed to own up to their own views.

Bush made other key gestures to indicate to the Right that he was one of them. In one of the first acts of his administration, he reinstated a U.S. government policy forbidding the use of federal funding in promoting contraceptive or abortion services abroad (the so-called Mexico City rule).[3] Bill Clinton had lifted the ban in 1993 on his second day as president, with great fanfare. Bush was letting his core supporters know that he shared their distaste for the notion that taxpayer dollars should be used to promote abortion, which he and they considered the taking of a life.

Perhaps even more notably, Bush took a key talking point from his campaign and made it the centerpiece of his social-welfare policy. He wanted to change federal law to make it permissible to funnel a variety of social services for the needy through churches, synagogues, mosques, and other religious institutions. Over time, many religious institutions came to believe that the initiative was a bad idea, because it would make them dependent on the federal government and force them to be subject to various regulations that might interfere with the frank pursuit of their religious missions.

Still, Bush was saying something significant, and profoundly pleasing, to those Americans in whose lives religion played the central role. He was saying he would not abide by the prevailing liberal doctrine that said the federal government needed to protect itself from the siren lure of religion. "The days of discriminating against religious institutions, simply because they are religious, must come to an end," Bush said at the National Prayer Breakfast in February 2001. Bush was placing *his* faith in the faithful— asserting his conviction that those who dedicate themselves to helping the poor because they want to live a godly life are the best and noblest among us.

If Ashcroft and the "faith-based" initiative were Bush's gestures toward the social conservatives, his tax-cut plan was his gesture toward those in the Republican coalition who concentrate on economic issues. Bush and his campaign team initially designed their ambitious, across-the-board tax-cut plan in 1999 as a means of countering Steve Forbes, one of his rivals for the Republican presidential nomination. Forbes was an advocate of an entirely flat tax—a very radical notion, but one that appealed to GOP primary voters because of its simplicity.

Bush found the counter to the Forbes challenge in the example of Ronald Reagan's plan to lower tax rates across the board. It was not as ambitious as Forbes's idea, but Forbes couldn't really attack it—because to attack it would be to attack Reagan, the most beloved Republican (among Republicans) of the twentieth century. Bush made himself acceptable to supply-side enthusiasts and Reaganites with his plan during the primaries and the general election. It was far from certain that Bush would stick with his campaign plan once he was president. But he did go with it, and go for it, and get it.

Here's how Bush's embrace of the Right helped him. Self-defined conservatives make up about one-third of the electorate and more than half of the Republican vote. Bush had watched his father alienate the Republican base during the Elder Bush's first three years in office and then suffer the consequences as the voters fled from him in various directions in 1992 (first to Pat Buchanan in the New Hampshire primary, then to Ross Perot in the general election). Bush knew he needed the base on his side and in his camp for good, and that there would be no better time to stake his claim to the base than at the outset of the adminis-tration. He surely knew that at various points during his admin-istration he was going to have to do things the base might not like. If he could convince conservatives that those things were done not because he wanted to betray them or suck up to the other team, but because he had no real choice, the ideologues in his own party would cut him substantial slack.

Conservatives had another important reason to look favorably

on George W. Bush: He humanized conservative politics again.
Bush imbued his core convictions with a sunny energy. It was
clear to Right-wingers that Bush was not acting out of cynicism,
but out of conviction. He deeply believed that the policies he was
advocating—from tax cuts to education reform to oil exploration
in the Arctic—were going to make life better for all Americans.

His cheerful, good-spirited progressivism represented a revolution in Republican consciousness. For even though Bush's views
were very much built upon the basis of the "Republican Revolution" of 1994, when the GOP won the House and Senate in a
landslide midterm election by running on a very specific and potent ten-point action agenda, he talked about them and thought
about them far differently. Bush was an advocate of tort reform,
securities reform, Social Security reform, the flattening of the tax
code, and better treatment of the U.S. military. All these had
been key provisions of the "Contract with America" that defined
the 1994 revolution. The reason Bush could run on the same
agenda six years later was that the revolution had been stymied;
most of the "Contract with America" agenda items were never
signed into law. Bill Clinton was partly to blame for that. But to
an even larger degree, the failure was due to the inability of the
Republican Party in Washington to make an ongoing, positive
case for change.

That failure was a matter of both style and spirit. The face of
the Republican Revolution had belonged to its architect, Newt
Gingrich. Gingrich was a brilliant tactical politician with a gigantic chip on his shoulder. He was inclined to speak about Republican domination of the American political scene in neo-Marxist
terms, as though his party's triumph had been and would continue to be a historical inevitability. But Gingrich didn't *act* like

it was inevitable at all. He didn't act like a winner, with the easy confidence and gregarious good will of a victor. Instead, he conducted his political campaigns as though he and the GOP were still backbenchers fighting a rear-guard battle against a more powerful foe.

The foe that haunted Gingrich wasn't just Bill Clinton, but the world of elite opinion that backed up Clinton and the Democratic Party. In his heart of hearts, and in the darkest heart of the conservative movement he represented, Gingrich never believed that he and the Right could triumph over the culturally dominant Democratic liberal Left that controlled television news, the op-ed pages of the major newspapers, and Hollywood. Gingrich whined and complained while he fought, as did Bob Dole, the GOP presidential candidate in 1996. Their bellyaching put off millions of Americans who might have been inclined to believe in their agenda. Bush didn't give his foes that kind of emotional power over him. And for that reason, conservatives already had cause to be grateful to him. This was more than a marriage of convenience. This was a meeting of the minds.

Bush did suffer one major political setback in 2001, when, in May, Jim Jeffords left the Republican Party. The Vermont senator would not become a Democrat, but he agreed to "caucus" with the Democrats in the Senate. With the Senate divided 50–50 after the 2000 election, Jeffords's decision instantly changed the balance of power in the institution that some—foolishly—call "the world's greatest deliberative body." Jeffords instantly became the poster boy for liberals. "Mr. Jeffords Blows Up Washington: A Quiet Yankee Sends a Loud Message to the Republican Right," proclaimed the breathless editors of *Newsweek* on their June 4, 2001, cover. They cast Jeffords's decision as a profound act of principle when in truth they were thrilled because he had flip-ped the Senate to the Democratic side—and got to use him as a club to beat Bush and the Republicans with. Bush had failed to move to the center and so had lost the Senate for himself; he only had himself to blame for the political disaster that was sure to follow.

There's no question that the Jeffords defection was a blow. As is often the case in politics, however, nothing is ever quite so simple as the media would have you believe. Jeffords had been aggressively courted by the Democrats for months. He had gone to the White House and demanded, as payment for his continued alignment with the GOP, a special provision in the new education law involving special education. The Jeffords provision would have cost—get this—$180 billion over five years. In other words, Bush and Company would have had to pay Jeffords a policy bribe totaling $36 billion a year to keep him in the fold. The price was just too high, and the White House knew that while the Jeffords defection would change things around in the Senate a bunch, it wouldn't represent a procedural calamity for the president. There were pseudo-Jeffordses in the Democratic Party as well, senators from Southern states, like Georgia's Zell Miller, who wouldn't switch parties but who basically voted with the Republican cau-cus. They would keep matters in balance, the White House thought.

It's hard to say what further difficulties Bush might have faced in the Senate had there been no September 11 to unite the coun-try and give him the kind of popularity he needed to get more things done. The Jeffords defection might have come to injure the president deeply over time. But as it turned out, the Senate would revert to Republican control soon enough. In the weeks leading up to the midterm elections in November 2002, Bush worked tirelessly to elect Republican senators. Previous presidents had tried, and almost always failed, to sway votes in nonpresidential races. Bush, to everyone's astonishment, succeeded. Republicans gained a net three Senate seats in the midterm election (and very nearly made it five), and the GOP pickup was almost entirely attributable to Bush himself. "Last night's results were amazing—as amazing in some ways as the '94 [Republican] takeover of the House," a senior White House staffer wrote in a confidential memo on November 6, 2002.

In politics you only have power to the extent that you punish your adversaries at the same time as you reward your friends. Bush succeeded in punishing many of those in the Democratic Party who made it their aim to stymie his legislative goals. The Republican takeover of the Senate stripped Democrats of all the perks a majority offers—committee chairmanships, the right to set the daily agenda, more staff, nicer offices, and the like. And where was Jim Jeffords then? Truly, a man without a country. Even the reporters lost interest.

★

In his first months, Bush demonstrated that a president with no true mandate and a nation divided following the most passionate partisan dustup in a century or more could establish an agenda and get things done. He did it by strengthening his own political base, speaking from conviction, advancing serious policy ideas, and doing it all with a smile on his face.

In the words of Carleton College professor Stephen Schier, editor of one of the first academic studies of this administration,

The primary project of the Bush presidency is the completion
of the political reconstruction of national politics, government and policy begun by Ronald Reagan in 1981. Examine
the features of the second Bush regime, and you will find
commitments, policies and tactics consistent with those of
Reagan and having as their ultimate end the lasting triumph
of Reaganite rule in national government: military strength,
tax cuts, enhanced executive power at the expense of Congress
and a stable electoral majority that prefers conservative Republicans. George W. Bush is centrally engaged in a project
of political restoration through tactically innovative means.[4]

This is, doubtless, what his partisan enemies fear most about
him.

Crazy Liberal Idea #3

Bush Is a Fanatic

The "project of restoration" that Steven Schier describes has fueled another of the ugly charges against George W. Bush. His opponents say he is a reactionary both politically and theologically, and that he is effecting a religious takeover of the United States and imposing his doctrinal fanaticism on the rest of the world. "The fate of America is in the hands of a little group of Protestant bigots," the prominent French journalist Henri Tincq writes in *Le Monde*. "George W. Bush demonstrates all the zeal of a convert. . . . The evangelical 'convert' is convinced to enter a small circle of the 'chosen.' He entertains a Manichean world view, divided between the forces of good and evil."[1]

The view from Paris is, as has been the case so often, echoed by Leftists in the United States. In the view of Annie Laurie Gaylor, editor of *Freethought Today*, Bush is "the most recklessly religious President we've seen. He's on a religious mission, and you can't divorce religion from his militarism. He believes in fighting righteous war."[2] The problem, according to Reverend C. Welton Gaddy, president of the Interfaith Alliance Foundation, is that "President Bush does not make the proper distinction, in my opinion, between his role as political leader and his role as religious leader."[3]

Alas for Gaddy, Bush has no role whatever as "religious leader." He is an elected politician who happens to be religious. As a political leader, though, Bush is informed by a powerful sense of right and wrong and good and evil. And it is one of the great tragedies of our time that many Western intellectuals have come to believe that any effort to draw distinctions between good and evil and then to take action against those who actively promote and execute evil acts is the mark not of a healthy society but of one ruled by a fanatic.

Indeed, several prominent scholars actually say that Bush is no different from the man whose followers carried out the bombings of the African embassies, the USS *Cole,* the World Trade Center, the Pentagon, and the Bali nightclub. "By describing his war on terror as a battle between good and evil," writes Karen Armstrong, the bestselling author of *Islam: A Short History,* "President Bush has unwittingly reproduced the rhetoric of [Osama] Bin Laden."[4] Similar thoughts have been offered by John Esposito, a professor of Middle Eastern studies at Georgetown University. Esposito says that Bush's use of religious language "is the mirror image of what Bin Laden has done."[5]

Yes, it is true that Bin Laden talks about good and evil and that George Bush talks about good and evil. There is one key difference, though: Bin Laden is evil and George Bush is good.

Bush's insistence on using the language of good and evil has infused the political debate with religious terminology in an unacceptable way, according to the bestselling religious scholar Elaine Pagels: "I have not previously seen a President use this kind of language as a way to shut down political discourse." Pagels was speaking five weeks before the beginning of the war with Iraq. Funny; I never saw any shutdown in political discourse. I saw protests across the country, op-eds attacking the president, politicians like Senator Robert Byrd saying he wept for the nation because it was going into Iraq. Nonetheless, since Pagels's opinion was not the prevailing view in the United States, it was obvious to her that Bush-the-fanatic was guilty of silencing his critics.

"Yes," Pagels acknowledged, "we do need the language of good and evil to talk about what certain events mean. But to use it to characterize whole groups of people, groups of countries . . . suggests we're not dealing with human beings on one side and human beings on the other side who need to negotiate and work out very difficult conflict."[6] It's comforting to know that people like Pagels can make distinctions so pure that *actions* can be considered evil even as the criminals who perpetrate those actions should not be. After all, we might have to negotiate with them, and where would we be if we called them "evil"? Well, in the case of Osama Bin Laden and Saddam Hussein, we'd be speaking the truth.

★

Just as the "amiable dunce" concept we explored back in Crazy Liberal Idea #1 is a liberal-Democratic trope dating back decades, so, too, is the Republican-president-as-fanatic line. It was used most successfully, and believed in most passionately, when Ronald Reagan was president. During the 1980s, in some Leftist quarters, it was argued that Reagan had a dual purpose: He wanted to

reverse decades of liberal social progress for ideological reasons—
and possibly to hasten the coming of a nuclear apocalypse for
religious reasons.

This might seem like a contradiction. After all, why bother
turning back the clock if you expect the world to end at any
moment? But the idea was bandied about very seriously. It was a
central theme of liberal and leftist critics of Reagan during the
1984 campaign, who argued that Reagan's confrontational posture toward the Soviet Union was a mark of a religiously inspired
fatalism, an expectation and even perhaps a hidden desire for a
nuclear conflagration. "It is hard to believe that the president
actually allows Armageddon ideology to shape his policies toward
the Soviet Union," wrote the editorialists of the *New York Times*
in 1984. "Yet it was he who first portrayed the Russian as satanic
and who keeps on talking about that final battle."[7]

Ronald Reagan got elected in part because of the support of
the Religious Right. Many in the Religious Right adhere to a
nineteenth-century Protestant doctrine called "dispensationalism."
As the conservative journalist Rod Dreher has explained in the
June 5, 2002, *National Review*, dispensationalists "proclaim that
the Bible foretells that the final stage of history before the advent
of the Antichrist and the Second Coming of Christ would see an
ingathering of Diaspora Jews from around the world to the Biblical land of Israel."[8] Following the "ingathering," dispensationalists believe, the Antichrist will rise and attempt to set up a world
government under his control.

Dispensationalists see the creation of Israel as the beginning
of their doctrine's fulfillment—and saw the Soviet Union's effort
to spread Communism throughout the globe as the rise of the
Antichrist and his world government. Soon after, the Anti-

christ will begin a seven-year war—Armageddon—during which he will, according to the book of Revelations, "rain down fire from the sky." Some dispensationalists have taken this to mean that the war between good and evil will be conducted with nuclear weapons. Finally, after much suffering, the forces of good will defeat the Antichrist and Jesus will return to Earth to set up his just and noble kingdom.

The Reagan critics figured it this way: Since the Good Guys win in the dispensationalist scenario, and the end result is paradise on Earth, Reagan and others must secretly crave a nuclear conflict!

There was at least one flaw in the anti-Reagan theory: Ronald Reagan was not a dispensationalist. Indeed, a few years after the issue was used against Reagan in the 1984 election, he shocked the world by proposing the banning of all nuclear missiles at the 1986 Reykjavik summit with the Soviet Union.

George W. Bush isn't a dispensationalist either (and in 2002, to follow Reagan's example, he actually reduced the U.S. nuclear arsenal by two-thirds). The president was raised as an Episcopalian and attends a Methodist church. He had a religious reawakening in 1985 and 1986, which began as a result of a conversation with dispensationalist minister Billy Graham. But Graham did not instruct Bush in dispensationalism. He merely asked Bush whether he was "right with God"—a phrase that, Bush has said, "planted a seed" in Bush's soul. Bush was not even "born again" in the sense in which most evangelical Protestants think of it. He was not rebaptized and never had an "Aha!" moment in which he communed with Jesus Christ. Bush is not, in other words, a theological follower of those who believe in the Rapture (the instant summoning to heaven of all those who have been saved by being born again), or the imminence of the end times featuring the coming of the Antichrist and a seven-year war. Nonetheless, Chip Berlet, a senior analyst for Political Research Associates, insists that "Bush is very much into the apocalyptic and messianic thinking of militant Christian evangelicals. He seems to buy into the worldview that there is a giant struggle between good and evil culminating in a final confrontation. People with that kind of worldview often take risks that are inappropriate and scary because they see it as carrying out God's will."[9]

Hobart University American studies professor Lee Quinby agrees: "What I hear is a holy trinity of militarism, masculinism and messianic zeal." God forbid! Not *masculinism*! "It does follow the logic of apocalyptic thought, which has a religious base but is now secularized in the militaristic mode."[10] Having difficulty understanding that last sentence? Basically it boils down to this: Quinby thinks George W. Bush is evil, to some degree, because he has a penis.

★

In the eyes of some Bush critics, the president's great failing is that he doesn't have the right *kind* of religious faith. It's a little startling to note that the most sustained argument in this line comes from Joe Klein, writing in *Time* magazine, who is neither by training nor by personal background a noted Protestant theologian. Klein discussed religion with Bush during his days as governor of Texas, when "his faith was humble and, well, soft. It softened his cowboy-preppie heart." But on the verge of war with Iraq, a war Klein opposed, Bush's faith was no longer acceptable because it was no longer, well, soft.

"What is disturbing about Bush's faith in the moment of

crisis," Klein wrote, is that "it does not discomfort him enough; it does not impel him to have second thoughts, to explore other intellectual possibilities or question the possible consequences of his actions. . . . George W. Bush's faith offers no speed bumps on the road to Baghdad."[11]

Now, Klein has no actual idea whether or not Bush's faith led to any "speed bumps." In point of fact, there were many "speed bumps" on the road to war. Bush began talking about the need for regime change in Iraq soon after September 11. The bombs did not begin to fall for another nineteen months. The debate over going to war was long and drawn-out, and his close aides tell me the decision to commit troops to Iraq was an agonizing one for him. That may be spin, I fully acknowledge, but it's also spin—facile, cheap, anti-Bush spin—for Klein to assert that the president's faith "does not give him pause or force him to reflect. It is a source of comfort but not of wisdom."

Thus, in Klein's view, because Bush's faith did not cause him to forgo war with Iraq, it's a *bad* faith. An unwise faith. This is a presumptuous and unwise argument. But it's not an argument made in bad faith. Klein, like Pagels and Gaddy and those who accuse Bush of being a mirror image of Bin Laden, truly believes that there is something pernicious in the fact that the president possesses deep convictions about right and wrong and is certain that the course he has adopted is the right course. They would all prefer a president who does not know his own mind, who does not believe in absolutes, and who follows their lead rather than the dictates of his own conscience. They prefer the equivocations of a Clinton to the certainties of a George W. Bush.

You don't have to believe the same things Bush believes about the centrality of Christ in our lives[12] to see what he saw in the

September 11 attacks—the first shot in a geopolitical battle between the forces of good and those who thirst for the blood of
the innocent. Indeed, Bush's clarity on the matter was shared in
the wake of the attacks by Jews and Muslims and atheists and
Christians alike—by people of good will who were not so immensely sophisticated (or so full of hatred of America) that they
were unable to understand that the threat posed by terrorists and
their mentors was something evil. And that the effort it will take
to end the threat is a righteous effort.

Clarity is not fanaticism. Bush hatred is.

4

Before September 11

Many Bush supporters believe that he only became a truly effective leader after September 11. In his splendid insider portrait, *The Right Man*, former Bush speechwriter David Frum goes so far as to argue that his ex-boss might have been doomed to mediocrity and eventual failure had it not been for the transformative effect of the terrorist war declared on the United States.

This notion gives September 11 its proper due as an epoch-making moment that changed not only Bush, but the United States and the world. There is no question that the event and this country's response to it have combined to make the Bush presidency among the most important in American history. The notion also has a bit of that Shakespearean Henry V kick, because it suggests that just as America awakened from a kind of self-indulgent innocence on September 11, so, too, did the country's callow president enter the forge and emerge as a piece of hardened and gleaming steel—a combination sword-and-shield ready to fight for the nation and protect it at the same time.

Satisfying as the melodramatic idea that Bush needed September 11 to teach him how to be president might be, however, it's not borne out by the record of the eight and a half months he spent in office before the Al-Qaeda attacks. For Bush had already demonstrated a formidable political savvy in the months between his inauguration and the September day that altered American and world history.

In sharp contrast to his predecessor, who transfixed the nation by masterfully scrambling to get himself out of trouble he had gotten himself into, Bush managed from his administration's first day to dominate the national debate. If Bill Clinton was his own worst enemy, George W. Bush is his own best friend. Indeed, the new administration's command of policy in its first few months was surprising, since those months are usually the period in which a new administration trips itself up by its own inexperience. In the first week of the Clinton administration, the White House had had to cope with a firestorm of its own making when then-spokesman George Stephanopoulos let it slip that Clinton was planning to change the rules governing gays in the military. This was a tricky battle the Clintonites really did not want to wage that early, as they had more pressing matters on their agenda. But they were loose-lipped and undisciplined. As a result of the passions they stirred up, both in the military and among Democrats in the Senate, they found themselves on the defensive and were ultimately unable to prevail on an issue they honestly believed was a matter of principle and fairness.

No such thing happened with Bush. Right from the beginning, in the winter of 2001, the new administration hit the ground running. With the exception of a brief and unpleasant blip when its first nominee for secretary of labor, Linda Chavez, had to withdraw because she had housed an illegal alien, the Bush administration suffered no fallout from its appointments and personnel decisions. Contrast that with the Clinton administration, which went through a comedy of errors over its many choices for attorney general (first Zoë Baird, then Kimba Wood, finally Janet Reno) or with the first Bush administration, whose first nominee for defense secretary (John Tower) went down in flames before the Senate.

There did come a moment of great political danger for the administration later in the year, a few weeks after September 11, when Enron went bankrupt. Enron had deep connections to the Bush administration, and in the two months preceding its collapse, the company's executives desperately sought to have the administration intercede in some way on its behalf. Had any Bush administration official lifted a finger on Enron's behalf, the consequences would have been calamitous. But no one did. (The only really questionable act of influence-peddling came when former treasury secretary Robert Rubin tried and failed to get a career Treasury employee who had worked for him to do something to help Enron.)

Though insinuations aplenty have been hurled about regarding the administration's closeness with big business, nothing has stuck. The administration's consultations with energy companies during its formulation of a new national energy strategy in the spring and summer of 2001 have become a centerpiece of anti-Bush conspiracy theories. But they never made a dent in the popular consciousness. Bush made no secret of his favorable view of the industry in which he'd gotten his start, and it's hard to claim that a man who openly discusses the importance of more aggressive oil drilling is somehow being unduly influenced. The influence peddlers haven't had to peddle their influence; *Bush already agrees with them.*

The proper functioning of the Bush White House in its early months was due in part to the close-knit nature of the president's staff. White Houses are usually snake pits. Factions form, battles are fought over access and control, newspaper leaks are used to tarnish and ruin members of rival factions—all in all, things get very ugly very fast. Not in the White House of George W. Bush. The officials in the top tier got along with each other. They had been working with each other closely for years in Texas and on the campaign and had long since worked out whatever problems they had with each other. Bush's core—national security adviser Condoleezza Rice, communications chief Karen Hughes, political adviser Karl Rove, speechwriter Michael Gerson, policy honcho Josh Bolten, and economic adviser Larry Lindsey—understood each other's weaknesses and strengths, quirks and abilities.

Or maybe it's better to say that if they didn't, they did know this: the president they worked for would not tolerate internecine strife. Bush places a premium on collegiality and good manners. He treats his staff well and with respect and expects them to do the same with each other. According to political scientist Martha Joynt Kumar, who specializes in presidential communications, "it's a highly compartmentalized White House, where people know what their tasks and responsibilities are. . . . It's been successful for them. It's brought them fewer mistakes at the beginning."[1]

Bush came into office pledging to change the tone in Washington, which had grown incredibly ugly and partisan during the Clinton years. Some of Bush's most senior aides have an ongoing discussion about whether he has succeeded. As evidence that there hasn't been much change, one aide points to the ugliness of the rhetoric of the Democratic candidates, the jihad against several Bush judicial nominees, and the demands for a witch hunt to determine the source of the revelation of a CIA agent's name in the summer of 2003.

Another argues that indeed Washington is a new place since Bush's arrival. There have been no serious congressional investigations into Bush administration malfeasance, and the president has secured Democratic support in the House and Senate more often than most observers expected he would. For his part, Bush rarely, if ever, offers a critical word about specific Democrats or about the philosophy and approach of the Democratic Party. As the veteran White House correspondent Carl M. Cannon reports in the *National Journal,*

> Former White House press secretary Ari Fleischer [says] that neither he nor current White House spokesman Scott Mc-Clellan has taken shots at opposition members of Congress, something that was common from the podium in the White House briefing room during Clinton's tenure. "Howard Dean criticizes Bush every day, but when he made that stumble on Israel, we stayed out of it," Fleischer said. "I mean, he served us up a softball on a tee—we could have whacked it out of the park. But Bush won't let us." Adds McClellan, "He really discourages personal criticism."[2]

In the months before September 11, Bush demonstrated that he could score complex legislative victories—and could even hold on to his conservative supporters in spite of the fact that he had to team up with the likes of the hated Ted Kennedy to win one. Bush had vowed during his campaign to make education the centerpiece of his administration, and he oversaw proposals for an education-reform program that included many features pleasing to conservatives of different stripes. For those who believe that introducing competition into public education is the key to repairing the broken American system of learning, Bush included school-choice and voucher proposals. For those who believe in tough standards, he added a provision demanding mandatory testing for children and their schools. For those who believe that the federal government's role in education is overly intrusive, Bush inserted a host of measures to end the Department of Education's micromanagement of local school districts.

His campaign's education-reform program was converted into a piece of legislation called the No Child Left Behind Act. As it made its way through Congress in 2001, the act was slowly but surely stripped of those elements allowing experiments in school choice and efforts to eliminate Washington micromanagement. The conservative Heritage Foundation declared that the bill had become "an expensive version of the status quo."[3] Even its one undeniably tough feature, the mandate for uniform testing across the nation, was opposed by many conservatives who believed it gave the federal government too much power over local school districts.

Many Republicans and conservatives complained that Bush had been forced to give away too much. And that he was spending too much (indeed, federal education expenditures have risen 61 percent during Bush's tenure). But he could not have gotten Congress to agree to the original reform package. Most of the heavy lifting on the No Child Left Behind Act was done before Labor Day 2001 (though the final bill would not reach his desk until the spring of 2002). In the end, according to leading education

reformer Chester E. Finn Jr., "the resulting measure is . . . a welcome improvement on current law but no revolution."[4] Bush and
his team had had to make a choice between principled failure and
partial tactical success on education legislation—between walking
away from a bill because it didn't do as much as he wanted or
assenting to a bill that offered him the opportunity to claim he
had done what he promised and put education at the center of
his presidential agenda.

★

The real centerpiece of his pre–September 11 presidency was his
$1.6 trillion tax-cut package—a plan that, as we've seen, first took
shape as Bush began campaigning for president in 1999, when he
decided to go for it largely to neutralize the threat posed by rival
Steve Forbes, the flat-tax advocate who had done unexpectedly
well in the New Hampshire primary in 1996.[5] Bush intimates
admit that he viewed his tax-cut proposal as primarily a useful
political tool in the general-election campaign—something positive to say and something to bash Al Gore with. It was only at
the very beginning of January 2001, fifteen days before he was
sworn in as president, that Bush got religion on the plan.

Forty business leaders were invited to the governor's mansion
in Austin to discuss the economy in a closed-door, off-the-record
session. And what they told the president was that things were
bad—very, very bad. The economy was about to fall off a cliff.
The stock-market bubble had burst. Consumer spending was
tanking. Business inventories were rising at a rapid rate, which
meant there would be no need for more manufacturing to replenish them. At that session, Bush concluded that his tax cut

was no longer just a useful talking point. It had become, says one aide, "a moral imperative." Government has little to offer a sinking economy besides tax cuts. Oh, there are jobs programs, but most serious people have lost faith in their efficacy. The only concrete help the government can offer is to extend unemployment benefits far beyond the thirteen weeks called for in law—something Bush has supported several times during his presidency.

Bush played his first big hand as president immediately. He announced that he wanted the tax cut he had proposed during his campaign. And he wanted *all* of it, all $1.6 trillion of it.

Now, nobody—and I mean nobody (on the political spectrum, that is)—really thought Bush would even *try* to get all of it. Ever since the big Reagan cut of 1981, tax-reduction proposals have gotten loaded up with goodies and chewed away around the edges until there's not all that much left. Immeasurably aided by a House and Senate dominated by Republicans (before the Jeffords flip-flop), Bush pushed and pushed and, in the end, got almost all he had asked for. He didn't get the top tax-rate cut to 33 percent; he had to settle for a reduction to 36 percent. But his determination was the key factor in his scoring a huge political success. Just as would later be the case with his education bill, Bush had kept his word.

★

Bush refused to accept conventional political wisdom on the need to seek consensus when it came to his tax-cut package. And in the realm of foreign policy and national security, Bush refused to accept the conventional wisdom about the overriding importance of international consensus. Bush had made it clear well before

9/11 that he did not believe, and would refuse to act as though, America would be best served by hewing to the official views of the so-called international community. He did not work for the United Nations, or the European Union. He worked for the American people and would do what was in their best interests. He based his foreign policy on the straightforward advocacy of American national interests and American principles, and he took terrific heat for it, in two areas especially.

In the late spring of 2001, Bush administration officials made it clear to Russia that the United States would presently withdraw from the 1972 Anti-Ballistic Missile treaty.[6] It was not, to put it mildly, a decision that earned him plaudits and garlands from the self-appointed leading lights of American foreign policy, from the turgidly hallowed halls of the Council on Foreign Relations to the chin-scratching corner of the New York Times op-ed page wherein resides the much-garlanded Thomas Friedman.

The conventional wisdom reflexively accepted by these so-called leading lights was that the ABM treaty remained vitally important— in no small measure because its existence restrained the United States from going ahead with the development of a system to defend the territory of the United States from the impact of a nuclear attack. There had been screaming about this ever since Ronald Reagan announced the creation of the Strategic Defense Initiative in 1983, back when the Soviet Union was still very much a threat.

Following years of powerful argument by international-law experts, the Bush administration said the treaty was no longer in the interests of the United States. It had been signed in 1972 with the Soviet Union—and the Soviet Union had long since ceased to exist. It was therefore geopolitically obsolete. The treaty was obsolete for technological reasons as well. It had been signed three decades earlier, before technological advancements made it possible to conceive of a potent defense against a missile fired at the United States. How could it make sense for the United States to remain vulnerable to such attack when it was increasingly likely that we might be able to protect ourselves?

The United States could have done what other nations do to avoid a scene: It could have nominally claimed to be sticking to the treaty while violating it in actuality. But the United States does not behave in such a manner. It makes agreements and it sticks to them. Alas, sticking to the ABM treaty as written was impeding the ability of the United States to design new systems to protect Americans from a nuclear attack by a rogue state.

It is depressing, but sadly true, that this argument did not sway much of conventional foreign-policy opinion—which, as I've suggested, supported the ABM treaty *precisely because* it tied American hands. Bush would not accept the contention that America's hands need to be tied by nations that are less free and less principled. Opponents of Bush's decision—domestic as well as foreign—seem to believe that American military and technological development actually represents a net threat to world peace. Bush does not. He believes American technological superiority offers yet another way to advance world peace and security by making it clear to rogue states that the United States is actively developing means and methods of negating any attack they might be considering.

For these reasons, the president believed it would be an abrogation of his duty to preserve, protect, and defend the United States if he refused to withdraw from the ABM treaty—which withdrawal, as it happens, was entirely legal under the terms of the treaty itself. What he did was the opposite of a rogue action. He was striking a blow for honesty and straightforwardness in the conduct of foreign policy.

So it was, too, when it came to his administration's announcement in June 2001 that the United States considered the 1997
Kyoto pact on global climate change "a dead letter," in the words
of Secretary of State Colin Powell. That decision brought the
wrath of Gaia on Bush's head. Every environmental group in the
United States condemned him. Worldwide he was savaged as a
despoiling, polluting brute who was (yet again) defying the will
of the international community.

What Bush did here was simply speak the truth. Kyoto *was* a
dead letter. It had been a dead letter years earlier. It had been a
dead letter even before Al Gore, then the vice president, signed
the accords with great fanfare at a big enviro to-do in Kyoto in
1997. Gore's signature was a legally meaningless act, as he and
Clinton well knew. Without the assent of two-thirds of the U.S.
Senate, no treaty is legally binding on the United States. And six
months prior to Gore's 1997 trip to Kyoto, the Senate had voted
95–0 in opposition to the terms of the Kyoto treaty because of
the devastation it would wreak on the U.S. economy. Not even
a single member of Clinton's and Gore's party supported passage
of the treaty.

That the United States was a "signatory" to the Kyoto treaty was
therefore sheer pretense on the part of the Clinton administration.
The administration refused even to send the treaty to the Senate for
an up-or-down vote because it wanted to continue to pretend it
held the status of a "signatory." Like the support for the ABM
treaty, international enthusiasm for the Kyoto provisions was due
in large measure to the restraints they sought to place on the economy of the United States. This country was to be held to vastly
more restrictive environmental standards than so-called second-
and third-world countries. According to Clinton's own Energy Department, the Kyoto accords would reduce real gross domestic

product by 4.1 percent, increase gas prices domestically by two-thirds, and raise the price of electricity by 86 percent.[7]

With his public acknowledgment that the United States was not legally bound by the Kyoto treaty, Bush was bringing an end to the pathetic fiction that the United States was in agreement with a document that would do spectacular damage to our own economy in the name of a disingenuous international effort to solve global warming by allowing nations other than the United States to contribute greenhouse gases to the upper atmosphere.

★

In the first months of his administration, Bush seized the initiative. He moved quickly and with determination on multiple fronts. The flurry of activity was heartening to his supporters and fellow Republicans—and put his opponents on notice that he knew what he wanted to do and how he wanted to do it. Two academics with distinctly unkind things to say about Bush, Ivo Daalder and James Lindsay of the Brookings Institution, write forthrightly about the leader they do not much admire: "Even before September 11, he demonstrated that he understood how to be an effective president to an extent that surprised even his most ardent supporters; he was decisive, resolute, and in command of his advisers."[8]

Future presidents will surely make a close study of Bush's first eight months in office so they can learn lessons on how to make policy from the moment they take up residence at 1600 Pennsylvania Avenue.

Crazy Liberal Idea #4

Bush Is Hitler . . . Only Not as Talented

Bush was aided in his first eight months as well by the fact that Democrats and liberals spent much of 2001 in a state of shock. They simply could not believe they had not prevailed in Florida. After all, the national vote tally—a number that may be meaningless constitutionally but was far from meaningless emotionally—showed Gore ahead by 500,000 votes (which was less than one half of one percent of the total).

One liberal writer, the perpetually enraged Robert Kuttner, tried to slap his party awake two weeks before Bush's inauguration: "What is the matter with the Democrats? They are rolling over in a blissful haze of bipartisanship, while George W. Bush appoints a hard-right Cabinet and pursues a hard-line program. . . . Are the Democrats on Prozac, or what?"[1]

Indeed, for months after the Florida recount ended, Democrats seemed spent and defeated. But the assertion that Bush had prevailed in a "bloodless coup" (Kuttner's phrase) continued to resonate in the fever swamps of the Left and in Europe, where contempt for Bush was flaring up everywhere. Kuttner had compared the "coup" to the goings-on in a South American "banana republic." In most quarters, though, use the term "bloodless coup" and you are referring to one man and one man only. These were the first stirrings of a soon-to-be-popular effort to analogize George W. Bush to Adolf Hitler.

Sooner or later, every Republican politician who comes across as a tough guy gets the Hitler treatment. In the 1980s, during demonstrations against the installation of medium-range nuclear missiles in Europe, protesters carried banners in which Adolf Hitler's moustache was affixed to Ronald Reagan's visage. In the 1990s, a self-described "street artist" named Robert Lederman plastered the Hitler moustache on New York mayor Rudolph Giuliani's face in hundreds of caricatures.

Such comparisons represent more than slander, more than libel. They are literally obscene. There are three major primary definitions of the word "obscene," according to the *American Heritage Dictionary*. The first is "offensive to accepted standards of decency and morality." Likening anyone to Hitler is obscene on the face of it unless the person in question has committed acts of genocide. The second is "inciting lustful feelings; lewd." The comparison is obscene because it does incite a certain type of blood lust in those who make it, a rhetorical lewdness. The third definition is "repulsive, disgusting." It should go without saying that likening these men to Hitler is repulsive and disgusting—especially when Ronald Reagan helped save hundreds of millions from the yoke of totalitarianism and Rudy Giuliani helped save New York from becoming an uninhabitable sewer.

Now it's George W. Bush's turn. Only, in his case, a few of

his critics do say the comparison is unjust. Hitler, they say, was more deserving of praise. "It's going too far to compare the Bush of 2003 to the Hitler of 1933," writes self-described "investigative reporter" Dave Lindorff on the Web site *Counterpunch.org,* "Bush simply is not the orator that Hitler was."[2] Very nearly the identical turn of phrase appeared online in the same publication a few weeks earlier, this time by Wayne Madsen, a senior fellow at the Electronic Privacy Information Center. "Hitler's oratory skills were light years beyond Bush's," wrote Madsen, who added that "Adolf Hitler would be proud that an American president is emulating him in so many ways."[3]

In what ways was Bush emulating Hitler? According to Edward Jayne, a professor of English at Western Michigan University, "Like Hitler, Bush curtails civil liberties and depends on detention centers (i.e., concentration camps) such as Guantanamo Bay."[4]

Yes, of course. There are six hundred prisoners at Gitmo, taken into custody after fighting the United States in battle in Afghanistan and taking part in a terrorist movement whose purpose is the mass murder of Americans. They are fed regularly, allowed to pray, allowed to exercise. The similarities to Hitler's concentration camps, where 6 million Jews and 1 million others were starved to death, gassed, and shot are just blindingly obvious, aren't they?

Maybe Gitmo isn't a Nazi concentration camp. Maybe it's more like one of Joseph Stalin's gulags, or a mixture of both, in the eyes of Carlos Fuentes, the most famous Mexican novelist of our time: "Just as Hitler acted in the name of the German Volk and Stalin in the name of the Proletariat, Bush claims to act in the name of the Northamerican people."[5] Well, no, Bush doesn't "claim" to act in the name of the American people. He *does* act in the name of the American people, according to the rules laid down in the Constitution of the United States. Nor does he act alone. Bush has twice proposed military efforts against Al-Qaeda and against Iraq. In both circumstances, combat was authorized by a majority vote of the other nationally elected representatives of the American people—those who serve in the House of Representatives and the U.S. Senate. Perhaps Carlos Fuentes, who never met a leftist dictator whose boot he wouldn't lick, is not terribly conversant with the workings of an actual democratic republic. Too bad for him.

Others are not quite so vulgar as to make the direct comparison to Hitler. Instead, they have taken to likening Bush and his staff to Joseph Goebbels, Hitler's chief propagandist. "It was all PR," says former CIA official Ray McGovern of the Iraq war. "Joseph Goebbels had this dictum: If you say something enough, the people will believe it . . . I think we all ought to be worried about fascism"[6] in the United States.

Andrew Greeley, the priest who writes fiction bad enough that his seemingly infinite number of rotten books should be imprisoned in a literary Gitmo, wrote in the *Chicago Sun-Times*: "Joseph Goebbels once said that if you are going to lie, you should tell a big lie. . . . What happens when people begin to doubt the big lie? Herr Goebbels never lived to find out. Some members of the Bush administration may."[7]

The Goebbels-like behavior to which both McGovern and Greeley refer is the case made by the administration that Iraq possessed weapons of mass destruction and was seeking to obtain a nuclear weapon. Their use of the phrase "big lie" indicates they believe Bush and Company knew such weapons did not exist but were so hell-bent on going to war they said so anyway.

If this is something McGovern and Greeley genuinely believe, then they have traveled beyond the reach of rational discourse. Or perhaps it would be better to say that they have placed themselves beyond the bounds of acceptable discourse simply by drawing analogies between George W. Bush and some of the worst people who have ever lived on this earth.

If the Nazi analogies go too far for you, how about an analogy to another Axis power? British columnist George Monbiot claims that "Japan went to war in the 1930s convinced, like George W. Bush, that it possessed a heaven-sent mission to 'liberate' Asia and extend the realm of its divine imperium." Thus, he writes, "[t]hose who question George Bush's foreign policy are no longer merely critics; they are blasphemers."[8]

You have to give Monbiot points for novelty in his analogy, even if the novelty is only slightly less hateful. Monbiot surely knows there is no "imperium" being set up here, either divine or secular. Japan annexed Manchuria and Korea, and would have annexed the rest of Southeast Asia had the war not prevented it. The Japanese did not want to liberate. They wanted to rule. The United States has no interest in annexing or ruling Iraq or Afghanistan or anywhere else. Right now, the United States is spending tens of billions of dollars to reconstruct Iraq so that it can stand on its own with a functional government that provides civil-rights guarantees to its people.

How evil.

★

The reason the Bush-as-Hitler analogy offers such a pleasurable frisson to those who write it (and even to those who won't write it but who surely think it) is that it is a politically pornographic version of the argument made by so many on the Left that Bush is an illegitimate president—"a selected dictator," to quote Ralph Nader.[9]

But even the hint of a comparison to Hitler's takeover in Germany is more than a little crazy. In the election preceding Hitler's swearing-in as chancellor in 1933, he received 37 percent of the vote to Paul von Hindenburg's 53 percent. In other words, Hitler was defeated in a *massive landslide.* In the parliamentary elections that took place a few months before the deal, the Nazis lost 15 percent of their seats in the Reichstag. The maneuver that landed Hitler the chancellorship was a game played by parliamentary powers confident they could control him.

In the 2000 election, by contrast, Bush and Gore ended up in a statistical dead heat in Florida. The arguments for and against the continuing recount were both strong. The Florida Supreme Court, dominated by Democratic appointees, backed the arguments that favored Gore and allowed a recount according to his wishes. The U.S. Supreme Court split along partisan lines and accepted the Bush team's argument that the recount had been designed in a way that violated the Fourteenth Amendment. Democrats were understandably enraged. Republicans were understandably relieved.

The recount struggle, the most exciting and dramatic political event in the history of American elections, was so all-consuming that the political class was burned out by it by the time it was over. But there's no question the shock would have worn off and the fight over Bush's legitimacy as president would have begun again in earnest had September 11 not intervened.

That national crisis changed everything. Bush conducted himself admirably in the eyes of most people, and at a time when the country felt itself under attack, it would have represented a threat to national security had the legitimacy issue reared its head again. The terrorist attacks inspired a national hunger for unity, even among those who believed Bush was unjustly and improperly resident in the White House.

The gradual emergence of the Iraq crisis in the summer of 2002 ended that surprising period of unity. It was as if the possibility of a second war so soon after the Afghan adventure had awakened Democrats and liberals anew from their ideological and partisan slumbers.

You could see it happening everywhere among the politically engaged. *Hey, wait a minute! Who is this guy? Why is he starting another war? We're Democrats! We're leftists! We only like wars when Democrats start them, and sometimes not even then! Bush shouldn't even be sitting in the White House, for Christ's sake!*

And so it all came rushing back, all the arguments and theories according to which a Republican-conservative conspiracy had installed a false leader. By the summer of 2003, with Bush's poll numbers dropping, Democrats began again to raise public questions about Bush's legitimacy. Bush "was not elected by the American people," as Democratic presidential candidate Carol Moseley-Braun put it during a debate in Baltimore in September 2003. "Bush stole the election," said Senator Tom Harkin at a campaign event in Iowa, where Bill Clinton said the Supreme Court "thought it was time for the minority to have the White House."[10]

Bob Kuttner got his wish, only three years late. Rhetoric challenging Bush's legitimacy was once again the order of the day—just as, in Europe, the Hitler analogies continued to fly. Indeed, the Hitler analogies have only been given greater weight by the

American liberal insistence that Bush became president due to a "bloodless coup."

The real insult of the analogy with Hitler, though, isn't to Bush. It's to the United States. Because, of course, if our leader is Adolf Hitler, then the United States is Nazi Germany. Which is precisely what Harold Pinter, the British playwright, had to say. "The U.S. is really beyond reason now," he said in June 2003. "There is only one comparison: Nazi Germany."[11] Thus does the hatred of Bush among European leftists reveal itself for what it really is: blind and unreasoning, ugly and unjust, foul and fetid hatred of America.

5

Master of the Political Game

George W. Bush is, as George Will has said, perhaps the most *personally* conservative individual to hold the presidency in modern times. He is a teetotaler, an ex-smoker, a relentless exerciser, a punctilious man who goes to bed at 9:30 every night after spending fifteen minutes reading an entry in his Tyndall House *Page-A-Day Bible.* He doesn't like movies with cursing in them. (He does swear like a sailor in private, as his father did, but will not take the Lord's name in vain.) And he prays daily for guidance.

This personal conservatism reflects a deep moral cautiousness. Bush, as he has repeated many times, "is mindful that we are all sinners." He usually says this when he wants to criticize himself (or his fellow conservatives when he fears they are acting holier-than-thou[1]). What he means is that he knows he is tempted by his own wildness of spirit—a wildness of spirit he managed to get under control only when he accepted Christ into his heart over the course of a year following that "planting of a seed" by Billy Graham in 1985.

The caution with which George W. Bush approaches his private life is not reflected in his presidential leadership. There he uses—as we've seen—boldness, daring, and surprise as potent political tools. This former owner of the Texas Rangers disdains the kind of policies he calls "smallball." He's a risk-taker who sets extraordinarily far-reaching goals and then fights for them as aggressively as he can. Knowing, perhaps, that he will be opposed by most Democrats (and much of anti-American opinion elsewhere in the world), he figures he might as well go for everything he wants rather than try to tailor a package that will be pleasing to those who are undecided or opposed.

By the same token, it is natural for him to play a patient and long game, to be willing to say the same thing over and over and over again, and to hold firm as he waits for fence sitters to get antsy, begin to worry, feel the pressure, and then at last come over to his side.

Here's how Bush plays the game. First, he will make a surprising overture—the staking-out of a far-out, go-it-alone, I-don't-need-anybody-I-can-do-this-all-by-myself position that draws expressions of outrage from his conventional opponents. For a time, he will continue stubbornly along the same far-out path and keep his opponents in a near-frenzied state.

Then comes the Bush Gambit: An apparent moderation of his position. He no longer insists upon his original far-out stance. He wants, he says, to work with those who oppose him to reach a solution. Whereupon his opponents believe that they have bested him, that they can enjoy a victory over him. Unfortunately, they've already lost. For at this point, his enemies have to choose.

They can choose to oppose him outright when the things he's fighting for are actually quite popular with the voters. Or they can support him, in which case they hand him a major victory. Either way, they're stuck. End result: A win for the president.

Perhaps this is where Bush's wildness of spirit, superficially tamed following his decision to quit drinking and smoking, has now found its expression. Certainly, that is what some of his opponents and adversaries believe; *Hartford Courant* columnist Alan Bisbort went so far as to characterize Bush as a "dry drunk," an accusation leveled as well by the *San Francisco Chronicle*'s Harley Sorensen. "A dry drunk, in simplest terms, is someone who doesn't drink but still retains many of the characteristics of a drinking alcoholic," writes Sorensen, who says Bush displays "exaggerated self-importance and pomposity, grandiose behavior, a rigid, judgmental outlook, impatience, childish behavior, irresponsible behavior, irrational rationalization, projection and overreaction."[2]

Forget, just for a moment, how truly insulting it is to refer to a habitual drinker who actually manages to quit drinking—a near-heroic act—as a "drunk." Any honest combatant in the ideological wars has to admit that the Bush-as-dry-drunk conceit is a cute theory. It's a clever way to dismiss the formidable sense of rectitude Bush has brought to other matters, such as the war on terror. His enemies have devised a pseudodiagnosis that turns Bush's moral strength into a disease. There's at least one major problem with it: reality.

It is rather easy to arrive at a judgment of Bush's political career, both because it has been so brief and because it has featured only two elected jobs. If he were genuinely a "dry drunk" (assuming there is such a thing), those so-called qualities would have found common expression during both his six years as governor of Texas and his presidency. But the political style of President George W. Bush has been entirely different from the political style of Governor George W. Bush. As president, Bush has shown an ornery determination, a willingness to go it alone in the face of extraordinary opposition. Governor Dubya was a conciliator, a dealmaker, a man who claimed his greatest political achievement was the relationship he struck with the state's most powerful Democrat, Bob Bullock.

Bush's conduct as president is not some unconscious reflection of a struggle with his internal demons. It reflects conscious choice, a series of practical decisions about how to get things done. To succeed in Texas, he had to govern in one way. To make his mark in Washington, he needed to go another way. And what he understood about Washington (a lesson surely learned during the thirty-six-day crucible following the November 2000 election) was that the only way he could succeed was by pursuing a bold course and using daring tactics along the way.

Though his stands may be bold and his tactics surprising, he takes and uses them in a diligent, patient, and disciplined way. He is biased on the side of ambition. He wants to fight battles that mean something, that are consequential. This is not to say that he is a radically unconventional politician. He isn't. Bush is content to compromise on matters that don't engage his passions. In 2002, he agreed to impose steel-import tariffs at the behest of Karl Rove—a violation of bedrock conservative free-trade ideology intended solely to strengthen his political position in the state of Pennsylvania for the 2004 election. That decision, one of the worst in his presidency, shows that Bush, like any other elected official, is not unwilling to sacrifice principle for expediency.

MASTER OF THE POLITICAL GAME

Among his talents is a knack for co-opting Democratic ideas, issues, and legislation, thereby laying claim to them and to the voters who are consumed by them—or at least neutralizing the damage they can do to him. This is best understood as a form of political jujitsu. At moments when Bush's opponents seem likely to best him by advocating a popular or politically useful policy opposed by the GOP, Bush will use their momentum against them by suddenly endorsing their efforts.

That is what happened with the campaign-finance bill drafted by Republican Senator John McCain and Democratic Senator Russ Feingold. The legislation was anathema to Republicans and conservative activists, who considered it a gross breach of First Amendment rights and an assault on the ability of private citizens to gather together to support and oppose certain policies. Democrats had been using campaign-finance reform as a weapon with which to bash Republicans for years. The GOP was in the pocket of big-money special interests, they claimed, and the only way to save the republic was by reducing the amount of money in politics and regulating political speech in the sixty days before a federal election. Their caricature of Republican politicians, Bush especially, threatened to become a dangerous political reality in the months following the business failures at Enron, WorldCom, and other firms that had played fast and loose with accounting gimmicks and the law—and whose corporate officials were major Republican donors to boot.

Bush let it be known he would sign any campaign-finance reform bill that Congress sent him. That instantly took the issue off the table for the Democrats, who could not claim any profound victory when the bill finally became law. Indeed, as time passed, Democrats began to realize that they had severely injured themselves and their party. The legislation banned so-called soft-money donations to political parties, but allowed an increase of $1,000 in individual "hard-money" donations to take the place of soft money.

The problem for Democrats is that the Republican advantage (and Bush's particular advantage) in "hard money" may be even greater than the GOP advantage when it came to "soft money." Bush raised $200 million in hard money for his 2000 campaign and will surely best that in 2004. Oops.

Bush has made use of a similar tactic on Medicare reform, accepting (in theory, as of this writing) expansive provisions that are repellent to many conservatives because he wanted his name on reform legislation to remove the Medicare arrow from the Democratic quiver and woo senior voters.

When Bill Clinton used this political technique, which his aide Dick Morris dubbed "triangulation," it drove Republicans into a frenzy of hatred. There is nothing more frustrating to party loyalists than this inventive form of ideological copyright infringement. "He's stealing our issues," I heard conservatives and Republicans whine in anguish throughout Clinton's presidency. These acts of "issue theft" upset them far more than the fact that important conservative initiatives—especially welfare reform, the single most important legislative act of the 1990s—were becoming law. Rather than feeling a grudging respect for Clinton for his recognition of reality and his willingness to stretch himself ideologically, they felt only burning rage. That seems not to make sense: After all, what really matters is what government does, not who gets the credit for it. But the real emotion brought on by political jujitsu is humiliation. When your adversary takes credit for your policy, you are unable to taste the sweet fruits. There are only gall and wormwood.

Still, Bush is driven far more by principle than by expediency, enough so that he deserves to be called a "conviction politician." All successful politicians find it necessary sometimes to trim their ideological sails for electoral gain. Ronald Reagan, the archetypal never-give-an-inch Cold Warrior, ought to have been a passionate supporter of the 1980 grain embargo imposed by Jimmy Carter on the Soviet Union as punishment for its invasion of Afghanistan. Instead, Reagan opposed the grain embargo because he wanted to win votes in farming states.

Bush's version of the grain embargo, as I've indicated, was the steel-quota decision—an ideologically wrong-headed choice. But the steel quota is not at all representative of his presidency. At his best, Bush goes all out for policies he believes will, first, be best for the country, then for his party, and, last, for his own political future.

And he does so in a singular fashion. Rather than building consensus beforehand in a series of quiet backdoor consultations, Bush asks for double what anyone would imagine he could. He does not offer his adversaries the chance to enter his confidence and then betray it to gain political advantage. Instead, he states his case as strongly as he knows how. He draws the howls and plaints and yells and insults of his adversaries, who find it nearly unbelievable he would act in a way so offensive to them. And then, in stiff-necked fashion, Bush refuses to alter his goals. He thereby presents his opponents with tough choices—and he presents those who are sitting on the political fence, trying to test the political winds, with nearly impossible ones. It boils down to this: They can go with him or they can oppose him. Time and again, they have conceded.

Once he has secured victory—in Iraq, for example—Bush's stiff-necked approach instantly gives way to tactical flexibility. If things aren't working right, he will quickly and unhesitatingly agree to change them. He'll change administrators, redirect policies, even seek United Nations support only months after abjuring it. His purpose isn't to dwell on the immediate victory or to insist on the rightness of his own day-to-day course but to secure the best outcome.

That also helps explain why, seven months after opposing the creation of a homeland security cabinet department, Bush changed course and supported it instead. Bush had thought at the outset that Tom Ridge, the Pennsylvania governor who left his important job to become the White House coordinator of homeland security, would be able to get all the departments of the federal government on the same page. After all, with the country under attack, surely even the bureaucrats could learn to compromise and work together.

Surely not. Bureaucratic prerogatives still dominated despite the national crisis. Bush and his aides determined that the structure of the homeland security effort wasn't working. The "dry drunk" of leftist legend would never have been able to see reason and change course. Bush, however, was able to put the nation's interests ahead of any vain wish he might have had to stick by his initial position.

On June 6, 2002, he proposed "the most extensive reorganization of the federal government since the 1940s." Bush aides say that both they and the president were continuing to learn on the job. They had hewed to conservative Republican dogma—which opposes the creation of new cabinet departments, indeed dreams of eliminating cabinet departments entirely. But that dogma didn't address the specific problem facing the country in 2002, and Bush felt he had to go beyond it.

Once the president determined that the reorganization was necessary to the task at hand, it became his priority. Given that Democratic Senator Joseph Lieberman had proposed just such a department in the wake of September 11, some complained that Bush had stolen their idea. And, they figured, because it had initially been a Democratic idea, the president would naturally cave in to the Democratic plan for the department. After all, they had watched as Expedient Bush, eager to fulfill his campaign promise of a mammoth new education bill, had allowed his ideological nemesis Ted Kennedy to lard his No Child Left Behind Act with goodies, and water down its more reformist elements. With the Senate still in Democratic hands in June 2002, the opposition party's leadership figured it could have its way with Bush on the Homeland Security Department just as Kennedy had had his way with the education bill. In particular, the Senate could insist that special protections be granted to the new department's workforce (government workers being the Democrats' most powerful voting bloc).

This time, Bush dug in his heels and said no. He would not compromise. He would not give in. In the fall, he made Democratic recalcitrance a campaign issue. Democrats "asked me to give up a power presidents have had for forty years, since John Kennedy was the president," Bush thundered, "and that is the ability to suspend collective bargaining rules in any department in the federal government when national security is at stake. In other words, I need to be able to suspend rules that prevent us from doing everything in our power to protect you. If some of the senators had their way, these rules would apply to the Department of Agriculture, but not to the Homeland Security Department. These rules would be okay for a department that deals with farmers, but not with a department dealing with your national security."

It was a bold and unexpected play, and few political pros thought Bush could really get much out of it. After all, he was trying to make an issue out of the organizational structure of a new cabinet department, and could anything be more boring? Voters wouldn't pay attention to the ins and outs of these things. After all, everybody, Democrats and Republicans alike, supported the creation of a new department in theory, so how could the fight over the internal details work for Bush?

It could, and it did. Bush the gambler bet that opposing him would go harder on the Democrats than they thought. He bet that the issue was worth hammering on in the ten days preceding the 2002 election. He staked quite a lot on this bet—a lot of time and the possibility that the American people would think he was using the homeland security issue as a partisan political weapon. And the bet paid off. Huge.

★

The combination of boldness and tactical flexibility makes Bush terrifically exciting to watch for those who view politics as a spectator sport. When the White House takes up an issue, Bush first asks his staff and advisers to tell him honestly what it will take— in terms of money, resources, time, effort, presidential involvement—to get the desired result. Once he commits, he does not back down or hesitate.

If he wants an education package, he wants a *major* education package—and he gets it. If he wants to fight AIDS, he wants to fight AIDS in the most *comprehensive* way possible. If he wants to help New York after 9/11, he need only have the figure $20 billion thrown at him before he speaks the simple words: "You shall have it."[3] In each of these cases, his daring caused his stunned enemies to freeze in place.

That was the case with cutting taxes. Twice. Liberals simply could not believe that Bush would begin the year 2003 by proposing dramatic new tax cuts when they were still expending breath attacking the cuts that had passed eighteen months earlier. They were so convinced by their own arguments, and so deaf to the ideas of others, that they seemed positively dumbstruck by Bush's audacity in disagreeing with them.

Nevertheless, propose new tax cuts in 2003 Bush did. And he did so because he believed that his first round of tax cuts had actually demonstrated their value. In August 2001, every taxpaying household received a $300 rebate check—an advance on its 2002 income-tax refund that was made possible by the just-passed tax-cut package. Bush's economic advisers believe that this one-time instant infusion of $30 billion worth of liquidity into the economy smothered the nascent recession in its crib. According to the hard data and the opinion of the Conference Board, the business group that has somehow been assigned the official job of determining whether the economy is in recession, there was but a single full quarter of recession—the second quarter of 2001, just before those rebate checks were mailed out. (The entire length of the recessionary period was eight months, from March to November 2001.)

Considering the economic dislocation brought about by September 11, particularly in the Northeast, the fact that in the very quarter during which the attacks took place the U.S. economy actually grew, when it had shrunk in size during the previous quarter, is an astounding fact. It's just that it's an astounding fact for which no one in the mainstream media is willing to assign Bush credit. He was actually blamed for a weak domestic economy when he might more properly have been praised for ensuring that the world economy did not sink into the slough of despond with the beginning of the war on terror.

The economy was sluggish throughout 2002, but it never dipped back into recession. Presidents are rarely, if ever, given credit for actions that may have staved off disaster, but there is a strong argument to be made that Bush's tax cuts did exactly that—preventing the economy from collapsing even as the stock market suffered from the combined shocks set off by the 90s bubble burst and the corporate-governance and accounting scandals. The combination of extraordinarily low interest rates (which function as an effective tax cut on the 70.1 million Americans who own their own homes[4] and could therefore refinance their mortgages at a sharply lower cost) and the Bush tax cuts kept the economy afloat.

Democrats, meanwhile, tried to assert that somehow the Bush tax cuts were *responsible* for the slow economy. This is a bizarre argument, because while one may think tax cuts are unfair or irresponsible or a threat to the continuance of good government, it's close to idiocy to believe that they might actually do *damage* to the economy. In fact, there was little way the Bush tax cuts could have any instantaneous effect—positive or negative—during the year 2002 (as opposed to the stimulating effect of the rebates in 2001 and the stimulating prospect of larger tax cuts to come). For the truth is that the tax-cut package was unfurling very, very slowly. Though its overall cost was estimated at $1.6 trillion over ten years, the total amount of the tax cut from the time the tax bill became law until the beginning of 2003 was approximately $55 billion.[5] That's during a period in which the economy's total output was somewhere around $16 trillion.

Thus, for the first eighteen months after Congress and Bush agreed to them, the tax cuts had a value roughly equivalent to one-third of one percent of the entire U.S. economy. In relative terms, that's close to nothing.

The decision to unroll the tax cuts over ten years was one of Bush's expedient political choices, made during the Republican primary season. Candidate Dubya did not want to be accused of trying to return the government to deficit spending after the surpluses that had accumulated in the last years of the Clinton administration. So chief economic adviser Larry Lindsey was told to "back-load" the tax-cut package. That is to say, most of the dollars returned to the American people would be returned past the year 2005. (By then, it was hoped, the economy would have grown significantly larger and therefore the tax cuts would not make trouble where deficits were concerned.)

Well, as the economy failed to grow much in 2002 following the single recessionary quarter in 2001, deficits did make their unwanted return. And they grew like Topsy, in part due to new spending required after September 11 (nearly 40,000 new federal employees as part of the Transportation Security Administration, a large part of the $20 billion promised to New York City, immediate and vast increases in defense spending to pay for the war in Afghanistan).

But the Bush budget deficit doesn't present the same kind of economic and political problem it once might have. Here's why.

The main fear engendered by deficit spending is that it will cause inflation. When the government is in deficit, it borrows money in large quantities from the U.S. Treasury in the form of long-term bonds. According to classic economic thinking, such borrowing creates competition in the market, because the government and the private sector are competing for the same investment dollars. Their competition drives up interest rates, which makes it more expensive for businesses to do what they have to do. Businesses then raise prices. Things get more expensive for consumers, and . . . Aaaah! Inflation!

In the decades that followed the conclusion of World War II, inflation was the great fear—the psychological torment of the American middle class. However, inflation has not been a problem in the United States for more than two decades. And in 2002, the great fear wasn't that a new round of inflation would destroy the U.S. economy. It was, rather, that there might be a worldwide *deflation*. Interest rates were at historic lows, which meant that banks and the federal government could barely give money away. The potential threat that haunted policymakers in 2002 was that what happened in Japan in the 1990s might happen here—a collapse in land values, commodity values, and the value of just about everything. Deflation is a kind of instant impoverishment out of which it is very hard to climb.

Bush decided to act in late 2002. He changed the players on his economic team and assigned his domestic team to come up with new ideas for stimulating the economy. He did not proscribe their research or efforts; what he wanted to know was what would *work*. Led by Josh Bolten, Bush's domestic-policy adviser (and later head of the Office of Management and Budget), his team began debating. They worried that they could not design a package acceptable to the Senate and the House—that the pundits would go after the president, liberal economists would emerge from their academic tombs to fulminate against any new policy, and that the administration would get trashed without anything to show for it.

They expressed these political concerns to the president. He answered with impatience: "Don't let's be negotiating with ourselves. You don't hear the word 'no' until it's spoken. Let's do something good."

So they considered all options, and came up with a package that accelerated many of the features of the 2001 tax cut and added a new element besides. It was a complex, multi-tiered proposal. To help generate disposable income for consumers to prime the economic pump, they sought to accelerate tax cuts that were to go into effect in 2004 and 2006—and increase the child tax credit by $400 a year. To boost the stock market, which was in the doldrums, they proposed ending the "double taxation" of dividends.[6] This would also have the effect of offering an incentive to corporations to produce dividends—thus tilting the stock-market balance away from pie-in-the-sky companies of the sort that garnered all the press in the 1990s and toward businesses that actually produce goods, employ people, and generate honest income. To aid small businesses and manufacturers that rely on those businesses to purchase their goods, the new tax proposal envisioned tripling the amount of equipment a small business could write off as "expenses" from $25,000 to $75,000.

The new Bush package was creative, clever, well reasoned, and far-reaching. And it was hugely expensive. When they were done, Bolten and the others tallied up the cost of their proposal—the amount it would remove from government coffers over ten years.

They determined it was $620 billion. (Later, the Congressional Budget Office did its own analysis and put the cost at $756 billion.)

Now, when we argue about the "cost" of a tax cut, we are arguing over something nearly impossible to determine—especially a tax-cut proposal oriented toward growth, as this one was. Its tangible cost may well be in the hundreds of billions over a period of time. But if the *effect* of the cuts is to accelerate economic growth, it really costs nothing. It pays for itself and more. The Reagan tax cuts, to take one dramatic example, created a deficit in the hundreds of billions. However, over the course of the twenty-year period inaugurated by those tax cuts, the U.S. economy as a whole literally doubled in size from $5 trillion to $10 trillion. The amount of money taken in by the government nearly doubled as well. Thus, those tax cuts didn't "cost" anything; they contributed to a radical increase in the amount of money received by the federal government.

Bush believes that economic growth is the solution to American domestic woes. He received news of the $700 billion price tag with equanimity. The plan was the right thing to do both in terms of tax fairness and to get the economy moving.

Even so, it was a knuckle-whitening moment in American politics. No president had ever done such a thing as following up a $1.6 trillion tax cut with a $756 billion tax cut. He'd get eaten up alive. The editorialists would blow a gasket. The think tankers would convene panicked conferences.

Perhaps, just perhaps, Bush was unfazed because he understood that the anger and grumbling of his critics might actually serve his political purposes. What the outraged critics and Cassandras would be telling the American people was that their president wanted to do something big and ambitious and striking—that he had a plan to help them and would not be frightened away by conventional concerns about its supposed parlous cost. He was their tribune, and he was working for them.

In the end, he got his 2003 tax cut—though once it got through the House and Senate, it was far different in structure from the bill he had sent up. Bush aides could barely contain their rage and disgust with House Ways and Means Committee chairman Bill Thomas, an incredibly arrogant politician from California who they thought hijacked their bill. But the White House embraced the compromise package, which did not eliminate the double taxation of dividends but did cut the capital-gains tax. And the new bill increased the child tax credit by $400. The credit was sent in August 2003 to all American households that can claim it—thus allowing a repeat of the instant stimulus offered by the 2001 rebate.

The 2003 tax-cut price tag is somewhere between $350 and $550 billion. Only a week after Bush signed the bill into law, the stock market responded with its first sustained rally in three years and the economy began its long-delayed turnaround.

★

The kind of daring Bush displayed with his tax cuts—especially in the second round—is rare in a politician, especially one who rises high enough to contend for the White House. Usually, the skills that make it possible for a man to maneuver his way to the point when he can consider a presidential bid are survivor's skills. A political survivor has to follow a path through the ineffably complex maze of voters, donors, interest groups, and media mavens. He must manage to be interesting without being offensive, exciting without being too provocative. It's a fiendishly difficult challenge, this "climbing to the top of the greasy pole," as the nineteenth-century British politician Benjamin Disraeli famously quipped.

You have to be daring to run for president, but when it comes to matters of policy, most presidential contenders act as though it is a mistake to be daring. They figure they'll make too many enemies and not enough friends. Just as the more plodding managerial fellow in the corporation often ends up as CEO, rather than the explosively brilliant idea man, so, too, in politics. That's why so many colorless and uninteresting men end up competing for the presidency, and why every four years Americans moan in disbelief at the choices they're presented with during primary season. *The most important job in the world and THIS is whom we have to choose among? Bruce Babbitt? Lamar Alexander? Paul Tsongas?*

And yet, for the most part, the men who succeed in winning the office are far from dull. The system favors the dull, but the voters don't. Richard Nixon may have been a headache, but he never was a bore. Jimmy Carter had a steely coldness all those smiling teeth couldn't hide. Then there was Ronald Reagan, a man so fascinating and unknowable that trying to encapsulate him drove his own biographer, Edmund Morris, into nervous collapse. And, of course, Bill Clinton, whose gargantuan personality will hover over American politics as long as he lives.

In one respect, Bush has a special advantage over many of his predecessors. He is not a career politician. He ran in only three elective races before his bid for the presidency, and won two of them. He did not spend twenty years in the game, as Bill Clinton and Richard Nixon and Al Gore (among others) had. His experience has not cowed him, has not made him afraid of taking risks. He can still gamble, because he gambled big on trying for the governorship of Texas, and won; and then gambled he could win the presidency from a standing start, and won. Gambling has worked for him.

★

Bush's greatest gamble was the war with Iraq. And it's instructive to note just how he got Congress and the United Nations to support him (at least in part). The war, which did not begin until March 18, 2003, became first thinkable and then doable as the result of a series of brilliant political plays Bush made during an eleven-week period beginning on August 26, 2002, and culminating on November 9, 2002. They won him a congressional resolution in support of a possible war, a U.N. resolution that supported a possible war, and a U.S. Senate dominated by the Republican Party.

On August 26, 2002, the administration of George W. Bush declared war. Not against Iraq, or Al-Qaeda, or the Taliban—but rather on those forces inside Washington and elsewhere that were staging a preemptive strike against the idea of going to war with Iraq. The declaration of war came in a startling headline on the front page of the *Washington Post*. "Bush Aides Say Iraq War Needs No Hill Vote," the headline read.

The impact of the headline was seismic, because of what had been going on in Washington and among the chattering classes throughout the month of August. Bush and his advisers had been absorbing all kinds of blows on the subject of a possible Iraq war.

Almost all the news stories in the mainstream media reported conflict inside the administration and open hostility to the idea from the armed forces. The *New York Times* had very nearly a story a day on its front page dedicated to the potential folly of such a conflict.

This attack from the Left was predictable. It was, nonetheless, deeply disheartening, because some of us on the Right had thought that after September 11, the knee-jerk opposition to the use of American power in pursuit of American national interests was a thing of the past.

We were wrong. Very wrong.

The crusading of the *New York Times* and others could be dismissed—and was—as partisan and small-minded. After all, Bill Clinton had threatened and executed military action against Saddam Hussein in 1998, when the Iraqi dictator essentially expelled U.N. arms inspectors, and received across-the-board support from those now opposing Bush.

What was more potentially damaging for Bush was the attack coming from Republican foreign-policy elders who had worked closely with Bush's father. Brent Scowcroft, who had been not only Bush the Elder's national security adviser but the coauthor of the former president's foreign-policy memoir, published an op-ed piece in the *Wall Street Journal,* titled "Don't Attack Saddam." Lawrence Eagleburger, who had served as secretary of state under Bush the Elder, joined Scowcroft in attacking the idea. The *New York Times* even claimed—falsely—on its front page that former secretary of state Henry Kissinger was opposed as well.

"August appeared to be a very bad month for the Bush team's effort to sell the Iraq war," wrote Joan Walsh in *Salon.com* in September. "Cheney and Secretary of State Colin Powell made dueling speeches contradicting one another, the president's father's closest advisors came out against the son's saber rattling, as did most world leaders, all while Bush was enjoying his customary month long vacation."

Bush's supporters fretted. Why was the administration refusing to go on the offensive? Why was he allowing his critics the upper hand? There was one crass indication that the administration's hapless loss of control of the debate had been a tactical ploy. Andy Card, the extremely efficient chief of staff who has always lacked a certain elegance as a public-relations salesman for his administration, told the *New York Times* on September 7, 2002, that "from a marketing point of view, you don't introduce new products in August." This was an unfortunate turn of phrase to use when talking about life-and-death issues, and it has been cited thousands of times by administration opponents to suggest that Bush and Company were approaching the Iraq issue in a sinister and frightening way. (This also helps explain why you rarely see Andy Card on television as a spokesman for the administration's positions.)

But the idea Card was trying to express was perfectly rational and appropriate. August is vacation time. Congress is out of session. The president is away at his ranch in Crawford. The American people are trying to find a way to relax before the school year starts. The administration did not wish to begin a major public discussion of a possible Iraq war until the president delivered his annual speech before the United Nations General Assembly, scheduled for September 12, 2002.

In truth, the debate had begun early because opponents of a possible war saw an opening—a moment in the discussion when they might dominate it. Grassroots opposition was growing in

Left-wing circles, which were heartened by the growing hostility
toward Bush in the European media. Antiwar organizers were
banging the drums, trying to call the Left into ideological battle
and seize the foreign-policy initiative from the administration by
reviving the notion that Bush was a reckless go-it-alone crazy person. This was not, politically speaking, an unwise strategy. Bush
had enjoyed stratospheric approval ratings on his handling of foreign policy for almost a year, and it behooved Democrats, liberals,
and leftists alike to try and cut him down to size. The philosophical justification for a possible Iraq war—the doctrine of preemption—was new and untested and seemed dangerous to many
in the foreign-policy establishment who tend to regard new ideas
with great suspicion.

If enough questions could be raised and doubt sown in the
minds of Americans, perhaps by the time Labor Day rolled
around, Democratic senators might actually be convinced to mus-
ter real opposition to the president's doctrine and his evident
ambition to try it out in Iraq. That opposition might resonate
with the American people, who needed to be taught that what
they considered an adventure in Iraq had nothing to do with their
fears about terrorism—and might represent a distraction from the
real war on terror.

After all, anyone who read the newspapers carefully knew that
there was deep conflict within the administration and among the
uniformed leaders of the armed forces about a war with Iraq—
whether it was necessary, whether we had the technical resources
to fight one so soon after Afghanistan, whether we could devise
a successful battle plan. Perhaps, those opposed to a possible war
thought, the intra-administration debates could be flushed out
into the open and Bush's dramatic policy advance could be
aborted.

As Nancy Pelosi, the Democratic leader in the House of Representatives, acknowledged ruefully just days before the beginning of the Iraq war in March 2003: "If the Democrats had spoken out more clearly in a unified vote five months ago in opposition to the resolution, if the people had gone onto the streets five months ago in these numbers in our country and around the world, I think we might have been in a different place today."[7]

In August 2002, the Senate was still controlled by the Democrats, albeit by a single vote. Sooner or later the president would have to go to Congress for a resolution supporting a war in Iraq. With Democrats in the majority in the Senate, it was conceivable that a groundswell of opposition could rise against Bush's idea and Bush himself. By making a big stink about Iraq early, the antiwar forces hoped they could commandeer the discussion and conduct it on their terms. Prowar forces feared they were succeeding.

Forced into early action, the administration began playing its hand.

The *Washington Post* story on August 26 reported that administration lawyers had looked into the terms to which Iraq had agreed at the close of the first Gulf War in 1991. According to the legal language, the peace between the United States and Iraq ever since was nothing more than a "cease-fire." The Persian Gulf War had never officially ended. And since almost every month Saddam Hussein did something to violate one of the sixteen U.N. resolutions dealing with the conduct of his regime, there was no question: Saddam Hussein *was* in breach of the cease-fire. The United States was within its rights at any time to reengage militarily with him.

The terms of the original resolution passed by Congress in January 1991 still stood. That's why Bill Clinton was able to drop bombs on Baghdad in 1998 without congressional authorization or United Nations support. And that, Bush's lawyers said, was why George W. Bush could go to war with Iraq without bringing the matter up before Congress.

The very idea was greeted with nothing short of horror in the world of conventional opinion. The president, said the Olympian editorialists of the *New York Times,* "seems to be under the illusion, supported by a recent memo from the White House counsel, Alberto Gonzales, that he can rely on the 1991 vote that authorized the Gulf War. . . . a decade-old vote is no substitute for the role the Constitution grants to Congress in taking the nation to war."[8] The solons on Capitol Hill howled as well, in private and in public. The president could not possibly conceive of going to war without congressional authorization. Such a decision would be a gross violation of the Constitution, an unwarranted seizure of power from the Congress—which alone has the power to declare war. What about consultation? What kind of seigneurial madness was this?

From that day forward, the administration moved ahead deliberately, making the case that Saddam Hussein posed a threat that needed to be taken with the utmost seriousness. The president privately assured congressional leaders that of course he would consult with them. But the overarching message was unmistakable: *We're going to do something. Your efforts haven't dissuaded us. In fact, we're willing to discuss doing something even without your say-so.*

On August 27, Vice President Cheney made a major speech to the Veterans of Foreign Wars, laying out the argument that Saddam Hussein had a thirst for nuclear weaponry: "On the nuclear question, many of you will recall that Saddam's nuclear ambitions suffered a severe setback in 1981 when the Israelis bombed the Osirak reactor. They suffered another major blow in Desert Storm and its aftermath. But we now know that Saddam has resumed his efforts to acquire nuclear weapons. Among other sources, we've gotten this from the firsthand testimony of defectors—including Saddam's own son-in-law, who was subsequently murdered at Saddam's direction. Many of us are convinced that Saddam will acquire nuclear weapons fairly soon." By "fairly soon," the vice president did not mean the next week, or the next month, or even the next year, as he made clear: "Just how soon, we cannot really gauge. Intelligence is an uncertain business, even in the best of circumstances. This is especially the case when you are dealing with a totalitarian regime that has made a science out of deceiving the international community."

We know now, because of the declassification of sections of the October 2002 National Intelligence Estimate, that the administration's best guess as to when Saddam would be able to obtain a nuclear weapon was sometime around 2006—three and a half years after the day of the Cheney speech. That fits precisely with the doctrine of "preemption" the president had laid out in June 2002 at West Point. It was time to oust Saddam *because* he wasn't yet ready to build a nuclear weapon—and because he would do so, given the opportunity. It was time to oust Saddam because, it was almost universally believed, he possessed chemical and biological weapons and would not destroy them as he had promised to do.

Cheney's speech had a major impact on the national discussion, for the reason that it focused attention outward. Before the speech, everybody had wanted to talk about Bush and Powell and Donald Rumsfeld and the Democrats. After the speech, everybody was talking about Saddam Hussein and terrorism and rogue nations and the threat of a combined assault by rogue nations and terror groups. So began the rollout—appearances on Sunday chat shows by major administration officials, a Bush meeting with British prime minister Tony Blair on September 7. The commemoration of the first anniversary of September 11 dominated the news as well, reminding Americans of the threat of militant Islam.

And then, on September 12, Bush went to the United Nations to seek that organization's support for a military effort to oust Saddam Hussein. This appeared, at first, like a concession on the president's part. It seemed to fulfill the demands made by the president's opponents, most importantly, Senate Majority Leader Tom Daschle, who had said the United States could not act against Iraq without the full support of the international community. The United Nations "will be a central factor in how quickly Congress acts," Daschle said. "If the international community supports it, if we can get the information we've been seeking, then I think we can move to a [Senate] resolution."[9] Democrats in the Senate began coalescing comfortably around this position.

Bush's landmark speech served several political purposes. First, he laid out the arguments for ousting Saddam Hussein from power, stressing both the dictator's continued defiance of every agreement he had made with the United Nations and his pursuit of weapons of mass destruction. It was a strong, sober, and straightforwardly worded brief, all the stronger for its directness— and it had exactly the desired effect, of focusing American attention on the threat posed by Iraq and the crimes committed by the Baathist regime.

Just as his administration had done with the leak about going to war without congressional authorization, Bush was putting potential adversaries here and abroad on notice. He let the U.N. Security Council know that as far as he was concerned, American action against Hussein was legal and moral—indeed, it was nothing less than a fulfillment of the United Nations' own demands and an enforcement of the United Nations' own dictates. Thus, he was not precisely seeking the *approval* of the United Nations. Rather, he was *demanding* that the international community step up to its obligations, and that the world body prove its viability and vitality. "All the world now faces a test, and the United Nations a difficult and defining moment," Bush said. "Are Security Council resolutions to be honored and enforced, or cast aside without consequence? Will the United Nations serve the purpose of its founding, or will it be irrelevant?"

By issuing this challenge to the United Nations, Bush let Senate Majority Leader Daschle and others who might oppose him in Washington know that he would not permit America to be held hostage by the Security Council. He would not give the United Nations veto power when it came to a vital issue concerning American national security.

Many Democrats didn't have the guts either to oppose the war or to embrace Bush. They knew war was probably inevitable, and they were hoping the United Nations would provide them cover from their own antiwar constituents. They wanted to be able to claim they were acting not because the president wanted them to but because of "world opinion." Then Bush, the former baseball-team proprietor, made it clear almost immediately that he was prepared to play hardball with the Democrats. On September 13, the day after his triumphant United Nations appearance, he was asked a question by Judy Keen of *USA Today*—a question he could easily have ducked. "Are you concerned that Democrats in Congress don't want a vote there [on Capitol Hill] until after U.N. action?" Keen asked.

Bush's reply was devastating: "I can't imagine an elected United States—elected member of the United States Senate or House of Representatives saying, 'I think I'm going to wait for the United Nations to make a decision.' It seems like to me that if you're representing the United States, you ought to be making a decision on what's best for the United States. If I were running for office, I'm not sure how I'd explain to the American people— say, vote for me, and, oh, by the way, on a matter of national security, I think I'm going to wait for somebody else to act."

The president had aimed a weapon of rhetorical mass destruction at the Democrats running for office in 2002. If they opposed him, declaring instead that the United Nations had the upper hand, he would use it against them in the upcoming congressional elections. Of course, Bush now made clear, he *wanted* congressional involvement: "My answer to the Congress is, they need to debate this issue and consult with us, and get the issue done as quickly as possible. It's in our national interests that we do so. I don't imagine Saddam Hussein sitting around, saying, gosh, I think I'm going to wait for some resolution. He's a threat that we must deal with as quickly as possible."

Message to Democrats: Fold.

Bush would never have gone to war without congressional approval, but the very fact that he could have even considered doing so gave him powerful leverage—especially after the American people didn't fall for the Democratic-liberal line that he was being irresponsible. He had played the political game perfectly. A mere four weeks later, well before the United Nations acted, the House and Senate voted to authorize the president to wage war against Iraq. And four weeks after that, the U.N. Security Council gave in as well with its unanimous vote for Resolution 1441, which called for war in all but name if Saddam Hussein failed to comply. The council voted just after the American people had given Bush a mandate for war in the results of the midterm 2002 elections.

The war with Iraq did not begin for another five months—a nerve-wracking five months, featuring demonstrations and all kinds of perfidious conduct at the United Nations by the French and the Germans. But Bush got everything he wanted and needed in that eleven-week period that began with the headline in the *Washington Post*.

★

The chronic "misunderestimation" of George W. Bush is rooted in the assumption that a man who once appeared to be incurious and inarticulate couldn't or wouldn't act on conviction. But the political skills he has demonstrated in his presidency make it unavoidable for a serious student of his administration to conclude that this *is* Bush's administration—and that the masterful use of all the political tools at the president's disposal are entirely attributable to Dubya himself.

Bush understood that the popularity he earned in the immediate wake of the September 11 attacks was his political capital. But where other presidents have tended to hoard their political capital, spend it frugally, and apportion it with miser-like care— most notoriously, his father, who frittered away a 91 percent approval rating by doing practically nothing from the day the Gulf

War ended until the day he left Washington—Bush believes that making bold investments with that capital is the surest way to keep it. Hoard it, and it dissipates. Put it on the line, and you will see it grow.

There is great risk—the risk of losing it all. But Bush doesn't seem intimidated or governed by a fear of risk.

That brings us back to the moral caution with which he lives his private life—a caution born out of the religious conviction that made it possible for him to turn his life around at the age of forty.

A close student of Bush's who works for him explains it best: "The president believes that we are called by God to do the best we can, to act responsibly and ethically and with good judgment. And then you rest in the comfort that God is in control, that history is not random, that He sustains the world that He has created. You do all you can—but you understand the results are not, in the deepest sense, yours to control."

The aide cautions that this conviction that God's purpose is transcendent "does not mean that you simply act and forget about things; there is a duty to persist in, and fight for, what is right. Justice is not self-executing; it needs advocates here on earth." But ultimately, "the president's faith allows him . . . a freedom to act and an inner comfort that others may not possess."

Crazy Liberal Idea #5

Bush Isn't Protecting You

Bush's inner comfort eludes his liberal critics, who twist them-selves into logical pretzels when it comes to criticizing his conduct of homeland security in the wake of the September 11 attacks.

On the one hand, they claim that the president isn't serious about homeland security. "It is clear," said Senator John Kerry, the Massachusetts Democrat and 2004 presidential candidate, "that a dangerous gap in credibility has developed between Pres-ident Bush's tough rhetoric and timid policies, which don't do nearly enough to protect Americans."[1]

On the other hand, they scream bloody murder when it comes to the most important effort Bush has made to secure the home-land—the passage and implementation of the USA Patriot Act, the post-9/11 legislation designed to make it easier to catch those fifth columnists who are planning attacks inside the United States. "The Patriot Act," writes Georgetown University professor David Cole, "in effect resurrects the philosophy of McCarthyism, simply substituting 'terrorist' for 'Communist.' "[2]

The inconsistency is typical of the way in which Left-liberal shibboleths have merged with simple partisan Bush-hatred to produce an argument in which Bush is the bad guy no matter what he does. The element of homeland security that Bush has supposedly mishandled, according to the critics, is the part they think ought to involve increased government regulation of private industry, a huge increase in the number of government workers, and a massive infusion of federal dollars into states and cities. The element of homeland security Bush has taken to dangerous extremes, in their eyes, is law enforcement, both civilian and military. The Lawyers Committee for Human Rights has gone so far as to say that the government of the United States is now "unbound by the rule of law."[3]

The Lawyers Committee and all those who speak so hysterically about Bush's handling of homeland-security issues are the ones unbound—unbound by rationality, the dictates of taste, or the capacity to make distinctions.

★

Senator Bob Graham, the Florida Democrat, based an entire presidential campaign on the accusation that America is in greater danger today than it was before 9/11. "We are less secure," his Web site's campaign literature stated baldly in September 2003. Graham's argument couldn't keep his campaign alive; it ended a few weeks later. But the argument remained ever-present among the surviving Democratic candidates. It was given its fullest expression by the Washington journalist Jonathan Chait in the March 10, 2003, edition of the *New Republic*. In an article titled "The 9/10 President," Chait detailed how Bush refused to go along with pieces of Democratic legislation that would have added tens of thousands of federal workers to search ship containers and the like. "Through passivity or, more often, active opposition, President Bush has repeatedly stifled efforts to strengthen domestic safeguards against further terrorist attacks. As a consequence, homeland security remains perilously deficient," Chait writes. "Bush's record on homeland security ought to be considered a scandal."[4]

You would think, reading Chait's article, that the measures Bush opposed were purely prophylactic, that they would be put in place solely to protect us by preventing a surprise attack inside the continental United States. But, in fact, the sorts of proposals supported by Chait, Graham, and others would create an entirely new regulatory system. Imagine entire sectors of the U.S. economy subjected to the kind of intense scrutiny now at work in airports and you get a sense of the overregulated America that Chait and others are seeking.

Take our ports. Every year, as many as 12 million cargo containers—some of them half the length of a football field and six stories in height—enter the United States by ship. We're talking about almost every single item of any substantial size imported into the United States, with a total value of $1.6 trillion.[5] Right now the Customs Service can search perhaps 2 percent of those containers.[6] Triple the size and the budget of the Customs Service, and its workforce could search perhaps 6 percent of them. That wouldn't represent much of an increase in security, but it would represent an enormous increase in the number of federal workers.

Chait is also upset with the administration because it did not go along with a proposal by New Jersey Senator Jon Corzine to treat the owners and managers of chemical and nuclear plants as though they are potential criminals—and as a potential cash cow for trial lawyers, another key Democratic interest group. Former senator Gary Hart charged in the *Washington Post* that "the White House was silent last summer while industry lobbyists scuttled federal legislation that would have required chemical companies to address their vulnerability to attack."[7] The requirement Hart is talking about would have authorized civil *and* criminal actions against plant managers and officials who supposedly weren't doing enough to secure their facilities. The logic of Corzine's (and Chait's and Hart's) position is that the courts should treat managers and owners of chemical plants who have done and are doing nothing wrong or illegal—and who have more to lose than any of us, including their own lives, if their plants should be attacked—as unwitting potential accomplices in acts of terrorism. That is foolish. Not only foolish, it is immoral, a dilution of the proper moral outrage against terrorist attacks. Such law would turn Americans against each other rather than allow them to focus on the true, external threat.

It is easy—easy and cheap and false—to go after Bush on the grounds that somehow he is kowtowing to business and placing the goals of capitalism above the security of the American people. The accusation supposes that Bush would choose to accept the deaths of thousands or hundreds of thousands of Americans because he doesn't want to bother his fat-cat friends or disturb his tax cut.[8]

Chait's damning but unjust criticism flies in the face of the passionate seriousness with which Bush has addressed the issue of homeland security and the war on terror. As we have seen, after determining it was necessary to do so, Bush did an about-face and supported the creation of a new homeland security cabinet department about eight months after the attacks. This, too, makes him the object of a Chait attack: Bush imperiled national security by failing initially to support the department, and then imperiled it still further once he saw the need for it. How so? Bush wanted the department run according to rules different from those sought by Senate Democrats. They held up his proposal because they wanted to do a favor for AFSCME, the labor union that represents public-sector workers, by giving collective-bargaining powers to the new department's personnel. To Chait's dismay, Bush turned their pandering to his own advantage: "By opposing the department's creation at first and then resisting any compromise, Bush created the very delay he bemoaned as injurious to the national defense—but gave himself a political issue with which to club the Democrats," he writes.

But the delay was *not* Bush's. The delay was caused by the Democrat-controlled Senate. And in any event, the establishment of the rules governing a new cabinet department—a department intended to function for decades as the first line of defense against terrorism—is vitally important for the proper conduct of the war on terror. Such a matter should not be rushed.

Bush was not the one living in the mindset of September 10. Rather, the Democratic senators who elevated the interests of AFSCME members over the proper functioning of the American government were the September 10 politicians par excellence. They saw a huge opportunity after September 11 and took it when they successfully pushed Bush and reluctant Republicans two months later to support the creation of the Transportation Security Administration, whose function was to enhance safety at American airports. The TSA is a new government agency with thirty-eight thousand new government workers.

Indeed, there has been a sustained effort by Democrats and liberals to use September 11 as an excuse to increase the size of the public sector, both in Washington and in states and cities. They do so mostly by invoking the need to support and aid "first responders," by which they mean police, firefighters, paramedics, and the like, who would have to lead emergency rescue efforts in case of another terrorist attack. Because of the horrifying loss of 343 New York City firefighters on September 11, the "first responder" now occupies a properly heroic position in the national consciousness.

The "first responder" has become a regrettable tool of Democratic propaganda against Bush. "When it comes to protecting America from terrorism, this administration is big on bluster and short on action," according to John Kerry. "It is a long way from 'Speak softly and carry a big stick' to a president who says 'Bring 'em on' and 'Dead or alive' and then leaves front-line defenders without the numbers and equipment they need to wage the war against terror."[9]

The charge is ludicrous. The Bush administration has proposed and secured $27 billion over five years for "first responders"— which is a colossal amount of federal money to fund duties that have historically been local in nature. It is necessary and proper that it did so. A terrorist attack in one city is an attack on us all, and the taxpayers in New York should not be (and have not been) forced to bear the burden of paying for the failure to destroy Al-Qaeda before 9/11.

But to Chait and others, $27 billion is chicken feed. In July 2003, the Council on Foreign Relations announced that the true amount necessary for first responders was . . . $98.4 billion. The council came up with the number after talking to local and state politicians (note that the council didn't round up to $100 billion, like any ordinary person would do, but kept its number at $98.4 billion deliberately to make it sound more precise). That's no surprise. No self-respecting local pol would choose to spend tax dollars on cops and firefighters if instead he could get the feds to pick up the bill.

Chait tries to indict Bush by saying that he rejected several requests for extra homeland-security money that came from inside his own administration. In Chait's reckoning, this means those proposals must have followed along conservative Republican lines, making Bush's rejection of them tantamount to lunacy. In truth, most if not all of those requests were off-the-shelf, wish-list sorts of things, the kind every cabinet department has ready to hand the White House at a moment's notice if there's the possibility of getting more money for its operation.

Here's the fact of the matter: In the first few months after 9/11, homeland-security spending rose by $40 billion (of which $20 billion is going to New York) in one fell swoop. The refusal of Bush and his staff to rubber-stamp every congressional and cabinet request for dollars wasn't and isn't irresponsible. It was and is prudent. The real criticism of Bush here is that, in the words of Paul Krugman in the *New York Times,* "the Bush administration . . . continues to subordinate U.S. security needs to its unchanged political agenda."[10]

The evidence for this dastardly conduct, Krugman says, is that homeland-security funding is flowing from Washington to all fifty states instead of being totally concentrated on urban centers. And, he says, Bush allowed or encouraged this to happen because he won the presidency in rural states and thus favors them over places like New York.

This attack is demented, even for Krugman. The structure of the federal government devised by the Founding Fathers 215 years ago is what's truly at issue here, not George Bush. Every state has two senators, whether it has 33 million residents, like California, or 500,000, like Wyoming. The result of this system is that there is always a fight about how to disburse federal money in a rational rather than a simply egalitarian manner.

"Any sensible program of spending on homeland security would at least partly redress" this problem, Krugman wrote. He's right. And the Bush administration *has redressed* this problem. By guaranteeing and following through on the promise that New York would receive a special $20 billion dispensation from the federal government, the administration succeeded in upending politics as usual. For which it has received scant credit from Krugman, who claims, "Republican lawmakers made it clear that they would not support any major effort to rebuild or even secure New York." This accusation is simply untrue. A few Republican lawmakers bitched about the special New York money, but the vast majority did not.

Krugman's real complaint is: Hey, what about New Jersey? "New Jersey pays about $1.50 in federal taxes for every dollar it gets in return," he whines, while "Montana received about $1.75 in federal spending for every dollar it pays out."

Krugman lives in New Jersey.

★

The key to Bush's domestic efforts to eliminate terrorism is the USA Patriot Act. The act makes it easier for law-enforcement officials to track and monitor the activities of suspected terrorists.

It is unquestionably the most outrageously caricatured aspect of the war on terror. Were you to believe its critics, the Patriot Act has given Attorney General John Ashcroft nearly unlimited powers to detain, whip, and draw-and-quarter anybody and everybody with a library card.

The critics of the act range from the American Civil Liberties Union on the Left to Clinton-bashing former representative Bob Barr on the Right. They have concentrated their ire on one small provision of the act, Section 215, that makes it easier for the FBI to obtain records from third parties as part of a terrorism investigation. As the criminologist Heather Mac Donald has written, "The ACLU warns that with section 215, 'the FBI could spy on a person because they don't like the books she reads, or because they don't like the websites she visits. They could spy on her because she wrote a letter to the editor that criticized government policy.' Stanford Law School dean Kathleen Sullivan calls section 215 'threatening.' And librarians, certain that the section is all about them, are scaring library users with signs warning that the government may spy on their reading habits."

Mac Donald is not a Bush-administration cheerleader; she was passionately opposed to the war in Iraq, for example. But her rebuttal is withering when it comes to criticisms of the Patriot Act. "These charges are nonsense," she writes. "Critics of section 215 deliberately ignore the fact that any request for items under the section requires judicial approval. An FBI agent cannot simply walk into a flight school or library and demand records. The bureau must first convince the court that oversees anti-terror investigations ... that the documents are relevant to protecting 'against international terrorism or clandestine intelligence activities.' "[11]

The Patriot Act's intent is simple, and its execution is entirely within the bounds of the Constitution. It merely removes roadblocks that had made it impossible for law enforcement to follow the complex trail of evidence that terrorists and their sympathizers leave around like bread crumbs in a forest. And its opponents cannot name a single instance—not a single instance—in which someone can claim to have had his civil liberties violated by the USA Patriot Act. Indeed, as the columnist Jonah Goldberg has pointed out, as of September 2003, Section 215 has never even been invoked: "Not only has the government never used 215, but the section doesn't even mention libraries—or any of the other secular holy sites allegedly imperiled by it."[12]

Bush's adversaries have tended to use the Patriot Act as shorthand for every security measure taken in the war on terror—in particular, the incarceration of Jose Padilla. Padilla, also known as Abdullah Al Mujahir, was a Chicago gang member who decided to join Al-Qaeda and traveled to Pakistan and Afghanistan, where he met Al-Qaeda officials. On his return to the United States, he was arrested at O'Hare Airport and designated an "enemy combatant" by order of the president. None of this had anything to do with the Patriot Act. The issue with Padilla has to do with whether an American citizen who does not serve in the armed forces can be transferred to the military-justice system using emergency wartime rules and held without access to a lawyer or a right to a speedy trial.

The Padilla decision has outraged many on the Right as well as the Left, because they fear it sets a dangerous precedent. An analogy is often drawn between the "enemy combatant" and Japanese-Americans who were rounded up into camps during World War II. The comparisons are insulting to the Japanese-

Americans, of whom more than a hundred thousand were un-justly detained. There is but a single person named Jose Padilla, and his detention is in no way unjust.

The *circumstances* of Padilla's detention, however, might be unjust. Those who say that Padilla should be charged in a U.S. court and tried under normal conditions have a strong argument. But they do not have a presumptive one. It's inarguable that Padilla was actively attempting to join Al-Qaeda and had contacts with the terrorist organization on the matter of detonating a so-called dirty bomb in the United States.

In the immortal words of Oliver Wendell Holmes, "Hard cases make bad law." Padilla's is the ultimate hard case. He was arrested, detained, and transferred to military authority under singular cir-cumstances. It is therefore unreasonable to extrapolate from the Padilla case to the entire edifice of post-9/11 justice.

But then, unreason is one hallmark of Bush hatred.

6

America, the Good Samaritan

Can't we do more?" George W. Bush spoke those words in a meeting in the Roosevelt Room, down the hall from the Oval Office, on June 19, 2002. He had just announced the details of a new program called the Mother and Child Transmission Initiative. The initiative was the second major commitment the Bush White House had made to the cause of AIDS prevention, cure, and treatment. A year earlier, the administration had created the Global Fund for AIDS Relief, which it had funded (with the help of Congress) to the tune of $1 billion over five years.

Bush, however, was not satisfied. He told his staff to bring him new proposals. A month later, the White House appointed a new AIDS advisor, a doctor named Joseph O'Neill who had worked on the issue at the Department of Health and Human Services (and who volunteered half a day each week to work with HIV patients at Johns Hopkins Medical Center in Baltimore). O'Neill was brought to the Oval Office for a few minutes of facetime with the president, a pro-forma meeting known in Beltway shorthand as a grip-and-grin. A session that was supposed to last for a few minutes stretched into forty—an unheard-of indulgence of time on the part of the rigorously scheduled president. "We have to start treating this like a public-health issue," Bush told O'Neill. He indicated the subject of AIDS had grown far too politicized. "Strip it free from all the other stuff. Treat it like a disease."

The president hadn't just been speaking off the cuff when he had said his administration should "do more." Once again, he wanted his staff to think big. He didn't want demonstration projects, starter projects. He wanted to commit the United States to a major effort to change the deadly facts on the ground in Africa. He had heard firsthand about the catastrophe from Senator Bill Frist, a doctor by training who went to Africa during his time off to minister to AIDS sufferers, and from some evangelical leaders who did missionary work there and had seen the horrifying effects of the runaway epidemic. Secretary of State Colin Powell was hearing about it from his ambassadors and was passing word along, as was Health and Human Services Secretary Tommy Thompson.

Nine months later, on April 29, 2003, in the East Room of the White House, Bush spoke before a crowd of Christian activists and others. In his speech, he urged Congress to vote within thirty days' time on the startling plan that had emerged from that first meeting in the Roosevelt Room. The plan: to spend five years and $15 billion in an effort to break the back of the AIDS epidemic in Africa and the Caribbean. It would be the most expensive and ambitious international public-health plan ever devised.

Bush concluded his remarks on that warm April day in a peculiar rhetorical fashion. He did not end on a note of hope, as one might have expected, but rather with reference to a Biblical parable. "Fighting AIDS on a global scale is a massive and complicated undertaking," he said. "Yet this cause is rooted in the simplest of moral duties. When we see this kind of preventable suffering, when we see a plague leaving graves and orphans across a continent, we must act. When we see the wounded traveler on the road to Jericho, we will not, America will not, pass to the other side of the road."

This allusion to the story of Jesus and the Good Samaritan, which appears in the Gospel According to Luke, was woven into the address at Bush's behest by chief speechwriter Michael Gerson (similar to a line from Bush's inaugural address). It was not just a grandiose attempt to echo the glory of the New Testament. In an extremely subtle way, Bush was simultaneously appealing to the rank-and-file within his ideological coalition and firing a warning shot across the bow of some of the leaders of that coalition.

He was explicitly framing his new AIDS initiative as an act of Christian charity, and the language he used was intended to resonate powerfully with the voters who make up the Christian Right. The president also knew that his expensive, revolutionary, and ideologically unorthodox proposal contained several details that were displeasing to some self-appointed leaders of the Religious Right. Indeed, his proposal had become something of a political football as activists of the Left and Right tore into it and whined about the way it violated their ideological sensibilities. He wanted to put his friends as well as his enemies on notice that he would be severely disappointed if they chose to oppose his plan. And he wanted to let his friends hear his warning by using language he knew they would understand—but which would, at the same time, sail over the heads of the religiously illiterate members of the mainstream media.

That's why he and Gerson chose to conclude his remarks rather abruptly with the tale of the Good Samaritan. As Jesus tells the parable, religious leaders encounter a wounded traveler. They consciously avoid him. Meanwhile, a poor traveler from a barbarian tribe does the right thing and helps the injured man. Jesus tells the story to demonstrate that merely occupying a position of high ecclesiastical authority doesn't confer moral authority on a person. A man has a responsibility to do good things if he wants to be good. What Bush was saying to the Religious Right leadership is this: *I want the United States to act like the Good Samaritan. If you oppose me, you will be like the priest and the Levite whom Jesus has made infamous for all time because of their inaction.*

And what *was* it Jesus said we should learn from the Good Samaritan? Just this: *Go and do thou likewise.*

Bush sent his message. The message was received. Yet nobody in the media wrote a story about how he had effectively and successfully sought to intimidate some of his own most prominent supporters.

★

What happened in the months between these two White House gatherings offers a revealing and heretofore untold tale of how the Bush White House, at its best, combines daring, vision, the capacity for surprise, and the willingness to think capaciously— and, as the cliché would have it, "outside the box"—on a matter the president insists on taking seriously.

Bush has repeatedly compared his AIDS policy to several of the most important humanitarian interventions of the twentieth century. "We are the nation of the Marshall Plan, the Berlin Airlift, and the Peace Corps," he said on May 27, 2003, in a speech at the State Department, where he was signing into law the very legislation he had demanded Congress put on the fast track a month earlier. "And now we're the nation of the Emergency Plan for AIDS Relief."

The Marshall Plan rebuilt the shattered cities and industries of Western Europe. The Berlin Airlift saved the free sectors of that city from Communist domination. And the Peace Corps was designed to unite American idealism and American know-how to help modernize the undeveloped world. These humanitarian interventions weren't simply examples of American generosity. They were also important elements of a complex Cold War foreign policy. Bush's AIDS initiative has a similar, although far subtler, place in the foreign policy of the United States after September 11.

Bush introduced his AIDS initiative in the State of the Union speech in January 2003.[1] "As our nation moves troops and builds alliances to make our world safer," he said, "we must also remember our calling as a blessed country is to make this world better. Today, on the continent of Africa, nearly 30 million people have the AIDS virus. . . . More than 4 million require immediate drug treatment. Yet across that continent, only 50,000 AIDS victims— only 50,000—are receiving the medicine they need."

The president continued: "A doctor in rural South Africa describes his frustration. He says, 'We have no medicines. Many hospitals tell people, you've got AIDS, we can't help you. Go home and die.' In an age of miraculous medicines, no person should have to hear those words. AIDS can be prevented. Antiretroviral drugs can extend life for many years."

Then came words that nobody expected him or any American

president ever to utter: "Ladies and gentlemen, seldom has history offered a greater opportunity to do so much for so many. . . . Tonight I propose the Emergency Plan for AIDS Relief—a work of mercy beyond all current international efforts to help the people of Africa. . . . I ask the Congress to commit $15 billion over the next five years, including nearly $10 billion in new money, to turn the tide against AIDS in the most afflicted nations of Africa and the Caribbean."

The notion that Bush would highlight AIDS at all in the State of the Union came as an enormous shock. After all, the nation was embroiled in a war on terrorism and on the verge of war with Iraq. Desperate though the situation in Africa was, few expected Bush to devote much time to any other foreign-policy topic. Perhaps Bush might mention the epidemic and the need to confront it. Perhaps he would pay lip service to a crisis that had been much in the news over the previous two years. But he didn't need to do much more than that.

Does that preceding sentence sound heartless? It's merely a realistic description of the demands made on a president and his State of the Union speech. Every humanitarian crisis in the world can't be mentioned, and every effort to address it can't be presented to the American people for their approval. There's just not enough time, even for the garrulous, laundry-list, grab-bags that all State of the Union speeches are.

Bush's AIDS announcement was even more of a shock, because the planning had been so closely held inside the White House—yet another example of how the discipline of the president for the most part flows down to his aides, who conducted their inquiries and helped design the proposal without even thinking of making a self-aggrandizing phone call to a reporter to claim credit. West Wing officials consulted very quietly on the matter and did not send it out to cabinet departments for what is called staffing. They kept it quiet, and not merely to keep the element of surprise, though God knows Bush and his people love to break their own news and not have it dribble out in leaks. They wanted to make sure that they could discuss the more controversial and difficult aspects of the proposal without being instantly subjected to political pressure from those in their own coalition. They understood they were going to have to enter a sector of the vigorously contested territory in the American culture war, and didn't want to invite hostile fire from the entrenched culture-warriors until they had a plan in place.

When Frist came to Bush in the summer of 2002 to make an appeal for significant American intervention on the matter, Bush told him point blank, "If you can show me this money won't go down the rat hole, I'm willing to make a serious commitment." It turned out that Frist could show Bush exactly that—and so could cabinet officers like Thompson and Colin Powell.

The Bush initiative is not based on wishful thinking or distorted by a sentimental fantasy about ending disease by throwing money at it. It's based on two salient facts and one important policy decision.

The first salient fact is that the cost of anti-retroviral drugs used to treat AIDS has dropped vertiginously over the past four years ("from $12,000 a year to under $300 a year," the president said in the State of the Union). That price drop made it possible for the White House to consider delivering them to millions of people without bankrupting the federal government.

The second salient fact is that there is now a proven model for the prevention of AIDS transmission in Africa—a program first developed and implemented a decade ago in Uganda that has shown dramatic results. The Uganda program deals with AIDS at every level of society—hospitals in the cities, regional medical centers in smaller communities, down to pharmacists on motorcycles who carry anti-retroviral drugs into the bush. The anti-retroviral treatment for those with AIDS and the aggressive intervention with newborns whose mothers have AIDS are joined together with a simple message the Ugandans call ABC: Abstain, Be Faithful, or Wear a Condom. The results have been a blessing. Fifteen percent of the population of Uganda had AIDS in 1991. In 2001, the number was 5 percent. Transmission rates have declined precipitously, and the only explanation for it is the ABC program.

Third, and perhaps most important, is that the White House chose as a matter of policy to focus its efforts, targeting fourteen countries, as well as Uganda, rather than the entire planet. They called it a "rifle-shot" approach, first adopted for the Mother and Child Transmission Initiative in 2002.

To do this, Bush needed to create an entirely new program. Existing efforts and funding streams were committed to a different, and by necessity less aggressive, approach to controlling the epidemic. The United Nations already had in place a brand-new Global Fund for AIDS Relief, to which the United States had already agreed to contribute $200 million a year for five years, or $1 billion in total (making it the largest benefactor of the fund by far). The Global Fund wasn't the right organization to manage the Bush initiative, and one can understand the reason just by looking at its name. The global scale of the Global Fund for AIDS Relief makes it an unwieldy effort. There are sixty countries receiving help through the United Nations' program. That money must be distributed according to the demands of U.N. politics. Outside of the United Nations, the United States itself has fifty different existing programs with individual countries to combat AIDS. Inevitably, because of the enormous scale, such efforts are more like slapping on Band-Aids than administering surgical triage.

With the new "rifle-shot" approach, the Bush team determined it would spend all $15 billion in the fourteen hardest-hit countries in the world—twelve in Africa and two in the Caribbean.[2] If the approach produced the sorts of results that have been seen in Uganda, the administration believed it could then convince regional powers in other places (China and Russia especially) to take responsibility for conditions in their own as well as neighboring nations. If "we whip it in those fourteen," Bush has said, "we will show what is possible in other countries."

The sheer magnitude of Bush's proposal—a direct commitment of $15 billion in foreign aid—was very nearly unprecedented. For a Republican president like Bush to stake the moral reputation of his administration on a gargantuan foreign-aid program is jaw-dropping. It is a deeply held axiom among thoughtful and knowledgeable conservatives that U.S. government handouts to third-world countries have been nothing short of disastrous for those countries—they lead to widespread corruption and graft and often leave the neediest in worse shape than they were before the handouts. If we climb down from the empyrean heights occupied by international-assistance skeptics such as Nicholas Eberstadt, one of the world's great experts on foreign medical aid, to everyday Republicans, we find among the ordinary GOP folk a profound hostility toward foreign aid of any kind on the grounds that it's nothing but a form of international welfare. And if we hate welfare here at home, we sure hate it even more abroad, where it isn't even flowing into American hands.

It's one thing to keep a program going for reasons of entropy, as Republicans always have in the case of foreign aid. It's quite another to commit billions in American taxpayer money for an entirely new foreign-aid effort.

This is yet another example of how far Bush is from being an orthodox conservative, following the prescribed ideological path blazed by intellectuals and activists. For the past forty years, conservatives have made the argument that, yes, America is indeed a "great nation," but that its government could not really do great things. Efforts to eradicate poverty in the Great Society only undermined families and did not lift the poor out of penury. The same was true of international-aid programs—our own, the World Bank's, the United Nations'—which too often had the perverse effect of strengthening dictators and pushing grandiose public-works projects, like dams, that had little positive economic effect and all kinds of unintended consequences, sociologically and ecologically. The best government could do, conservatives have long believed, was get out of the way—remove barriers to free trade, lower taxes to stimulate economic activity, and deliver the good word of the free market to nations that know it not.

What explains Bush's initiative? It is a matter of conscience and conviction for him. "How will history judge us," he said privately in a meeting with White House staff in December 2002, "if we don't act? If you can save millions of lives, how can you not do it? How can you stand by and watch?" In a speech he gave in the Ugandan city of Entebbe in July 2003, he stopped asking rhetorical questions and gave the answer instead: "I believe God has called us into action. I believe we have a responsibility. . . . We are a great nation, we're a wealthy nation. We have a responsibility to help a neighbor in need, a brother and sister in crisis."

In stating that the moral responsibility of the rich to the poor could best be fulfilled in this case by the direct intervention of the U.S. government, Bush was emending a conservative political doctrine four decades in the making. Moreover, by committing large-scale resources to Africa, Bush was emending his own expressed view of the continent's lack of importance. During an interview in 2000, he was asked by PBS's Jim Lehrer whether Africa "fit in to your definition of strategic interests." Bush replied, simply, "No." He went on to say: "It fits into my definition of economic interest, and that's why I try to promote free trade."[3]

That view corresponded to the general opinion on the Right. Serious foreign-policy intellectuals aligned with the Republican Party were so concerned in 2000 about getting the country to pay attention to the potential threats to the United States being posed by militant Islamic states and China that they tended to consider Africa a side issue—raised in American politics most commonly as a Democratic sop to African-American voters. The best you could do for Africa was trade with the countries there.

Clinton administration officials had occasionally raised the notion that the AIDS epidemic might represent a threat to national security, but they could never quite formulate the reason why—other than that instability on the continent would create a nightmarish humanitarian situation. Awful, to be sure, but there have been humanitarian crises every decade in Africa and, to speak in the most cold-blooded terms, those crises have really not affected the security of the United States.

The effort to connect AIDS and national security was greeted with derision on the Right. Until September 11, that is, when it began to be understood that if political instability in Africa led to a corresponding rise in Islamic fundamentalism and militancy—especially in oil-rich Nigeria—the consequences could be dire. There was already a powerful precedent: Osama Bin Laden had made common cause in the 1990s with the government of Sudan. In the end, Sudan couldn't do much for Bin Laden and Bin Laden couldn't do much for Sudan. An Osama-friendly Nigeria, on the other hand, could pose a horrendous threat. Worse still, the decentralized nature of African countries might provide Al-Qaeda with exactly the sort of cover that it could use to find a new home base. If the United States helped bring AIDS under control in some of these places, the gratitude their populations would feel toward the United States—and the social calm that would prevail—might prevent the emergence of wide-scale terror networks in Africa.

White House officials insist this foreign-policy argument was not present at all in their discussions of the AIDS plan—that for Bush, the whole matter is strictly humanitarian. I have no reason to doubt the sincerity of their view, or Bush's humanitarian sincerity. But the fact is that every decision the president has made since the terrorist attacks has been informed by them. He may not have discussed the foreign-policy implications openly. They were there, though, as always.

★

Still, the most profound surprise of all was simply that a conservative Republican president was declaring an offensive in the war on AIDS. You cannot understand the politics of AIDS in the United States without first understanding the nature of the cultural divide that has split Left and Right since the 1960s. In the years since 1973, when the Supreme Court mysteriously uncovered an unlimited right to abortion in the U.S. Constitution, the Republican Party has been the political home for moral traditionalists disturbed by the increasing vulgarity and libertinism on display in the United States. These traditionalists believe in limits on human behavior, sexual behavior especially. Many, though not all, of the traditionalists find their transcendent truth in the Judeo-Christian ethic—and the limitations it places on sexual self-expression. Those limitations are unambiguous, particularly when it comes to homosexuality.

The emergence of AIDS in 1981 created a new battlefield in the culture war. The Left used the national sympathy for the victims of AIDS to further the cause of gay liberation. They treated AIDS as though the disease were a manifestation of the nation's deep-seated hostility toward homosexuality, and acted as though its cure could be found only when homosexuality was given equal status with heterosexuality. For the Right, the epidemic was a manifestation of the cost of 1960s-style sexual license. Since AIDS was the result of the open expression of homosexual hungers, it could also be understood as a cautionary lesson about the fatal dangers of gay liberation.

When the gay-rights movement chose to use the AIDS epidemic to advance homosexual liberation, it practically forced the Republican Party into a defensive, even hostile stance. It was universally acknowledged that a new disease had arisen that needed to be fought, and its victims needed treatment, care, and understanding. But to morph that necessity into a demand that traditionalists surrender their deep convictions? To insist that religious believers simply rewrite the Bible to fit the fashions of the moment? That was impossible, especially for fundamentalist Christians who take every word of the Bible as literal fact. What was even more offensive to the traditionalists was the suggestion that those who spoke out against the homosexual lifestyle were like human versions of the virus that was sickening and killing so many. They were being accused of immorality and murder when they had done nothing to deserve such slander.

No disease has ever been more politicized. As the epidemic exploded, so did the political ugliness. It became common on the Left to blame Presidents Ronald Reagan and George Bush the Elder for the disease's tragic spread. They were routinely accused of doing nothing to stop it—even as the federal government was spending vastly more per capita on AIDS than on any other disease. Of course, the vitriol had less to do with AIDS than with gay rights, which was *the* vanguard issue for social revolutionaries seeking to expand the limits of permissible human behavior. And while religious conservatives did invoke the Christian doctrine to "love the sinner and hate the sin," in the case of homosexuals, many of them admittedly spent far more time hating the sin than loving the sinner. Such is the nature of the culture war, which like all wars causes the combatants to dehumanize the enemy.

★

However, gay rights weren't the focal point of the culture war in the 1980s. Abortion was. And in the case of Bush's AIDS initiative, these two battlegrounds would both come into play.

The greatest victory scored by pro-lifers during the Reagan-Bush years was a policy that came to be known as the "Mexico City rule." In 1984, in Mexico City, Ronald Reagan announced that federal grant money spent abroad by the Agency for International Development (U.S.A.I.D.) could not be given to private groups that promoted "family planning" in foreign countries. This

was a purely symbolic victory for the pro-life forces; the amount
of money involved was minuscule. Then, in 1992, the Supreme
Court took up the constitutionality of abortion in *Casey v.
Planned Parenthood*—and refused to overturn *Roe v. Wade*, the
1973 decision that gave abortion the standing of a constitutional
right. A few months later, Bill Clinton ascended to the presidency.
His first official act in office was to void the Mexico City rule.

The hopes of the pro-life movement were dashed. Abortion
was here to stay. At that moment, abortion receded as the primary
battleground in the culture war—and gay rights took its place.
For some traditionalists, the gay-rights movement represented the
most radical threat to their understanding of society's core values
in human history, especially as the gay-rights agenda was shifting
into a full-fledged effort to redefine the meaning of parenthood
and family to include same-sex couples. At the same time, the
movement was aggressively pursuing the explicit inclusion of homosexuals among those specific minority groups protected in law,
which led traditionalists to fear that the homosexual lifestyle was
soon going to be given *preferential* treatment.

The battle lines divided neatly. Liberals and Democrats supported the gay agenda. Conservatives and Republicans did not.
And the culture-warriors—the organizations that collected names
and raised money and did work at the grassroots level either supporting or opposing the cause—had their rallying cries. Liberal
culture-warriors were thrilled to have a new civil-rights cause,
especially one that was greeted with such distaste by conservatives.
It made them feel better about their own virtue. Conservative
culture-warriors were also driven by a conviction about the vir-
tuousness of their struggle against the revision of all traditional
social mores.

George W. Bush came to office with no ties to and no support from the organized community of AIDS activists in the United States. Far from it. Just as they did with his predecessors and other Republican politicians, the AIDS community tarred Bush with a broad brush. In their eyes, Bush was and is a retrogressive, reactionary, anti-gay monster no matter what he does. He may have "pledged a lot of money to fight AIDS," admitted Michelangelo Signorile, the journalist who invented "outing," in the *Advocate*, but that is insignificant compared to the evil Bush intends to do to homosexuals. "George W. Bush is not only lackluster on gay rights—or even mildly damaging; he is the single most dangerous president we've had on the issue, one who could very well do more harm to gay individuals and their civil rights movement than any other president in history."[4]

In the days following the announcement of the $15 billion program, AIDS activists still could not assimilate the news or grant Bush the credit for having elevated the issue to a central place in the American political debate. Salih Booker, the executive director of Africa Action, told the *Boston Globe* that the whole thing "could turn out to be a cruel joke. Not only doesn't it give any major new money in fiscal year 2003 and 2004, but it undermines the Global Fund as the main vehicle fighting AIDS."[5] Booker was flat-out wrong, as is every single person who continues to peddle this fiction. The Bush proposal features $2 billion in new money in fiscal 2004, and the amount given each year will increase as the five years goes along and the program becomes increasingly capable of absorbing the dollars. And the Global Fund had only been the main vehicle fighting AIDS for a year, so Booker was really shedding crocodile tears.

Some in the international-assistance community hailed the president's words. "You'll think I'm off my trolley when I say this, but the Bush administration is the most radical in a positive sense in its approach to Africa since Kennedy," averred Bob Geldof, the rock musician who created Live Aid in the 1980s.[6] But there was mostly stony silence from those who think the paint-by-numbers liberal caricature of Republicans is an accurate portrait.

Indeed, when Republicans act in ways that invalidate the caricature, activists sometimes get angry. Republican Bill Frist, the senator (now Senate majority leader) who was the leading voice in his party for expanding funds to counter AIDS in Africa, had excitedly told the president before the State of the Union speech, "You just saved hundreds of thousands of lives." The Bush proposal was the fulfillment of Frist's hard-fought efforts to get his party to address the matter with seriousness of purpose. But for those who use AIDS as a political weapon, Frist was a villain, because he threw his support behind Bush's plan rather than a more conventional approach, which had been outlined in a piece of legislation Frist himself had cosponsored the previous year with Senator John Kerry. Rather than being saluted for his work on behalf of the $15 billion, Frist was greeted by demonstrators outside his home and blasted by a leading AIDS organization, which issued a press release headlined "Sen. Frist Sabotages Key AIDS Initiatives."[7]

Instantly, it was back to AIDS politics as usual—and in the first few months of 2003, those politics threatened to hinder or derail the Bush plan. Conservatives called the White House, demanding that the "Mexico City rule"—which Bush had reinstated in 2001—be expanded to cover the new initiative. They could not bear the thought that a group like Planned Parenthood might end up administering some of the AIDS money, and wanted the

White House to go along with them. The White House said no. It was one thing to oppose Planned Parenthood's family-planning ideology. It was quite another matter if Planned Parenthood wanted to involve itself in an effort to halt the spread of AIDS.

Some social conservatives believed Bush had betrayed them because his embrace of Uganda's ABC plan meant that he was supporting the widespread use and distribution of condoms—yet another relic of the culture war. The very word "condom" was charged with symbolic meaning dating back to the 1980s, when liberals had strongly advocated that the government hand out free condoms in the United States to teenagers to halt the spread of AIDS. Conservatives believed this would destroy their efforts to convince youngsters and others that they could and should abstain from sex altogether—not only to avoid disease but to escape the lure of libertinism.

The problem with symbolic wars is that the combatants always end up obsessing over the symbols themselves rather than the context. That's what happened with the condom question. Condoms were indeed an important part of the Uganda strategy, but only a part—one leg of a tripod. The element most stressed by ABC was the "A" for "abstinence." In second place was the "B" for "be faithful." Condoms—the "C"—came last.

The legislation creating the Emergency Plan was written with extraordinary care to ensure that the private organizations involved were required to follow the ABC system precisely. That meant Planned Parenthood would have to preach and promote abstinence as the primary method of avoiding AIDS. (The White House did insist on a "conscience" clause for those religious bodies, the Catholic Church in particular, for whom the distribution of condoms constituted nothing less than a sin. The clause allows them to participate and to bring in other organizations to deal with the condom issue.)

By late April 2003, after phone calls from the president to some fence-sitters, and an extraordinary number of meetings involving the president, the legislation Bush wanted had passed the House and was awaiting action in the Senate. Most conservative organizations had reconciled themselves to the plan. Those inclined to oppose it had been overwhelmed by the new political reality Bush had created when he asked himself what history would think, what God would think, of him if he did not choose to end the fruitless ideological standoff on the issue of AIDS.

Once again, Bush's efforts represented a way to escape the restrictions of the culture war to find a way forward for the United States and the world.

Crazy Liberal Idea #6

Bush Wants to Bankrupt the Government

George W. Bush's $15 billion effort to cure AIDS in Africa is the most dramatic, but hardly the only, example of the president's embrace of government spending as a means of curing social ills abroad. Most famously, of course, there's the $22 billion he has secured to help with the reconstruction of Iraq and Afghanistan.

Bush has sought significant increases in federal outlays here at home as well. Overall, domestic spending has risen by 21 percent during the Bush administration. As the journalist and blogger nonpareil Andrew Sullivan writes in an essay highly critical of Bush published in *Time*, "Spending on education is up 61 percent; on energy 22 percent; on health and human services 22 percent; on the Labor Department a massive 56 percent."[1] And this doesn't even take into account Bush's support for a prescription-drug benefit, which would be "the biggest expansion of government health benefits since the Great Society,"[2] according to Nancy-Ann DeParle, who was the administrator of Medicare during the Clinton years. The cost is nearly inestimable—the administration says $400 billion over ten years, but entitlements like a prescription-drug benefit have a way of growing astronomically and unstoppably.

All this has alarmed conservative leaders. "The debate about how conservative Bush is, which began when he walked on the national stage in 1999, has been renewed,"[3] writes Ramesh Ponnuru, senior editor of *National Review,* the magazine that practically created present-day conservatism. Rush Limbaugh, the dean of conservative talk radio, considers Bush's government largesse the most disappointing aspect of his presidency. Limbaugh sees it as a moral and spiritual capitulation to big-government Democrats. "Some of this government spending has been part of the 'new tone,' " Limbaugh told his radio audience in September 2003, and "some of this has been designed to reach out, to extend the friendly finger of friendship to the Democrats and say, 'Hey, see? Don't hate us.' "[4]

Bush has given philosophical justification to his free-spending ways with a remark that really went beyond the bounds of any known conservatism. "When somebody hurts," he said on Labor Day 2003, "government has got to move." The idea that government exists to alleviate the pain of the American people is the underlying philosophy of New Deal liberalism. Limbaugh immediately went on the air and declared that he feared his fifteen years of broadcasting conservative ideas had all been for naught. One Bush aide tried to put the president's conduct in context by saying Bush's philosophy was "an activist, reforming conservatism that recognizes it's sometimes necessary to use the power of the government to change the status quo."[5] But that was cold comfort for those who believe Bush's abandonment of fiscal restraint is a betrayal of conservative principle. If you want to know what conservatives think, you have only to ask, or read what they write. They will tell you whether someone is hewing to conservative principle or not. In this case, Bush has failed a conservative ideological litmus test.

But Bush-haters can't accept what they read. They won't believe what conservatives are telling them. They are certain the whole thing is a sham, a fraud, a farce. They think Bush has a long-range goal, a dastardly scheme so clever and twisted that it might almost convince them he's neither an idiot nor a puppet but rather a schemer of Machiavellian proportions. "The underlying strategy is all too familiar," writes Princeton University professor Paul Starr in the *American Prospect*. "Instead of challenging popular liberal programs directly, the Republicans are creating fiscal conditions that make those programs unsustainable."[6]

Starr calls this the "Bush Bankruptcy Plan." It works as follows: By cutting taxes and increasing government spending at the same time, Bush is following the same program as Ronald Reagan in the 1980s. By taxing less and spending more, Republicans succeeded in "dominat[ing] national policy for a decade," even though they created a "fiscal disaster." Starr conveniently fails to mention that Reagan's "disaster" included ninety-two consecutive months of economic growth and the doubling in size of the U.S. economy. But no matter. This supposed "disaster" had to be dealt with, and in Starr's reckoning, Republicans made sure that Democrats were the ones who had to deal with it. "It was a Democratic Congress that began to rectify the problem," Starr writes, "forcing the elder George Bush in 1990 to accept a tax increase in a concession on his part to fiscal prudence."

Now see if you can follow his logic. George Bush the Elder

agrees to a tax increase (though the fiscal prudence in the budget deal had little to do with the tax increase and far more to do with the spending limits placed on the Democratic Congress). George Bush the Elder then loses the presidency in 1992, a defeat that places the White House, the Senate, and the House of Representatives all in Democratic hands for the first time in twelve years.

Boy, that was some great political scheme.

And now Bush's son is back at it, according to Starr's gnarled argument. It all works in phases, you see. "In the first phase, Republicans gain control of the national agenda through tax cuts that drain the Treasury," Starr writes. "Then, trying to prepare the ground for new initiatives,[7] Democrats enact responsible tax increases that hurt their own popularity, leaving them unable to carry out their positive agenda and setting the stage for a fresh round of tax cuts."

Starr continues in a tone of real bathos: "It's a great script for Republicans. They get to play Santa Claus while Democrats get to play Scrooge. Ultimately the Republican strategy unravels, as no government can keep cutting taxes and raising military spending indefinitely. But by the time the Republicans lose an election, there's no money to spend, and conservative policies are effectively locked in."

Oh? So why then has Ponnuru complained that "no federal programs have been eliminated, nor has Bush sought any such thing. More people are working for the federal government than at any point since the end of the Cold War. Spending has been growing faster than it did under Clinton"?

And yet Starr is still claiming—try and stay with me here—that by supporting increases in government spending and effectively endorsing liberal social programs that are anathema to conservatives, George W. Bush is trying to "lock in" *conservative* policies.

Starr is not alone in this peculiar interpretation of reality. Bush "is trying to gut every program providing for social, economic and environmental justice,"[8] writes Berkeley professor Arthur I. Blaustein in *Mother Jones*. Bill Moyers, the doyen of PBS, decries the "right-wing wrecking crews blasting away at social benefits once considered invulnerable . . . I think this is the deliberate, intentional destruction of the United States of America."[9] Correct me if I'm wrong, but doesn't a "wrecking crew" usually try to smash things rather than give them more money? Many Right-wingers are upset with George Bush precisely because he *hasn't* taken a wrecking ball to the federal government.

And another thing, Bill Moyers: If Bush and Company deliberately destroy America, where exactly do you think they will go once they're done and presumably find it necessary to seek out another country to destroy deliberately? How about France?

Of course, the policy the Bush-haters despise has nothing to do with government spending. Complaining about Republicans "gutting" government is another tired old cliché, and the fact that it's simply untrue in this case (as in most cases) doesn't keep them from saying it or believing it.

No, what they really, really hate are the Bush tax cuts. They hate the tax cuts because, well, they hate tax cuts. If you cut taxes, by definition, people in the upper tax brackets will pay out a smaller percentage of their income to the federal government. This is something liberals simply cannot abide. The tax-cutter's riposte is this: If you cut taxes and the wealth of the upper brackets grows as a result, they will end up sending more money to Washington even if they get to keep a greater percentage of their income. This is mathematically, statistically, and factually indisputable. So the issue for liberals really isn't whether government should have more money. It's really that the well-to-do should have a considerable amount of their money expropriated by government because it's plain unfair that they have so much of it.

Oh, and the tax cuts have another, more diabolical purpose, say some Bush-haters: They are designed purposefully to shift the tax burden in the United States away from the wealthy and onto the back of the middle class. This isn't just because Bush and his evil rich friends want every filthy cent they can get their grubby hands on. No, it's for political reasons—to force middle-class Americans to become Republicans!

This is the theory of Joshua Micah Marshall, an occasionally sensible liberal pundit who sadly slipped through the cracks of political reality and had to be fitted for an ideological straitjacket after he published an article titled "The Post-Modern Presidency" in the September 2003 issue of the *Washington Monthly*. "Republicans had come to view progressive federal taxation as the linchpin of Democratic strength," Marshall writes. "The more the tax burden shifted from upper-middle-class and wealthy voters to those of the middle class, the more average voters would feel the sting of each new government program, and the less likely they would be to support Democrats who call for such programs."

In other words, the Bush tax cuts were "designed to turn more voters into Republicans, particularly the middle class." So Marshall is essentially arguing that middle-class voters are increasingly Republican because Republicans have *raised* their taxes! And that they vote against Democrats who actually want to pass programs that will help them!

Here we have political lunacy at its Looney-Tuniest. In the

first place, middle-class federal income taxes have not increased. The federal income taxes of the middle class have been *lowered* as a result of the Bush tax cuts. And the argument that the middle class is paying more in federal income taxes than the wealthy isn't correct. According to the Internal Revenue Service, the top 50 percent of taxpayers in the United States paid 96 percent of the federal income taxes in the year 2000.[10]

It is true that taxpayers across the country have been getting hit with property-tax and state and local tax increases due to the slowing national economy. This, too, is somehow Bush's fault, according to *Boston Globe* columnist and *American Prospect* coeditor Robert Kuttner: "He sits in Washington, crowing about the benefits of his tax and spending cuts as if states were part of another planet."[11] Yes, now we are even to blame George W. Bush for the collapse in state tax receipts due to the economic slowdown that began at the tail end of the Clinton presidency.

According to the blogger Mickey Kaus, Kuttner is commonly called Crazy Bob by those who know him. Alas, Crazy Bob has a lot of company when it comes to crazy ideas about Bush's economic policies.

7

Thinking About the Unthinkable

On the morning of September 11, 2001, George W. Bush was told by his chief of staff, Andy Card, that America was "under attack." He was sitting in a classroom in Sarasota, Florida, in a chair built for a prepubescent child. For half an hour thereafter, the Emma E. Booker Elementary School turned into a command post as the president and White House officials struggled to figure out what was going on in New York, whether the White House and the Capitol were at direct risk, and what measures to take against commercial aircraft still in the air and unaccounted for. Photographs show an anxious Bush reading a document as he stands on a rug on the classroom floor decorated with the letters of the alphabet. His left foot covers the letter "Y."

There could have been no more plangent an irony than the setting in which Bush first heard the banshee wail of the new millennium. He had gone to Florida to promote childhood literacy—the most innocuous and controversy-free of subjects, the sort of issue you can dwell on when there's nothing much else going on. A president who talks frequently about education is a president who is governing during good times. If you're a voter and you're not especially worried about the security of your job, or a crime wave, or inflation, or a looming global threat, you have the luxury of imagining that the most important issue facing the country is the quality of your child's (or grandchild's, or neighbor's child's) schooling.

Not to discount the profound importance of a good education and the wondrous virtues of literacy, but shouldn't we expect a little more from a president than that he personally intervene to ensure that our children read at grade level? After all, if you care about it so much, you can take steps yourself to ensure it happens.

Like his father, Bush had said he wanted to be the "education president." But at the instant when Card leaned toward his boss and whispered in his ear, Bush could be the "education president" no longer. Of course he would continue to speak about education during his term, as he would about other matters—like a prescription-drug benefit—that had once seemed to be so pressing, so vitally important, so . . . well . . . so enticing when pollsters asked questions about them. But now he was a president at war.

He made the transition smoothly, but that transition was, and remains, far more difficult for other politicians. Indeed, you could sense in the months following September 11 a desperate hunger on the part of Washington elected officials to return to the old familiar debates with which they had grown comfortable before the attacks. In a collective fit of blind madness that overtook pollsters and politicians and media types alike in the summer of 2002, Washington even managed to convince itself that terrorism was no longer the key issue on the minds of American voters.

Polling suggested that matters like a prescription-drug benefit and the condition of the economy were more important to Americans than the threat of terrorism. In August of that year, according to a Pew poll, 39 percent of Americans said the president should focus primarily on the economy, while only 34 percent said terrorism should be his primary concern.

These data gave Democrats the sense that they had a chance to woo voters by speaking about topics other than national security and terrorism during the 2002 election campaigns—and that they would pay no price for opposing the president's wishes on the structure of the new homeland security cabinet department he was proposing. But when the dust cleared after November 5, 2002, even the blind could no longer fail to see the truth. Bush and the Republicans had clobbered the Democrats in the midterm elections, picking up seats in the House of Representatives and taking back control of the Senate, because national security and the war on terrorism were just about the *only* issues on the minds of voters.

How can we make sense of this peculiar contradiction between the polling data and the bald truth? It's as simple as this: Ask people what they are worried about when it comes to their health, and they'll say cancer. They won't say that what really concerns them is the ability to draw the next breath; it wouldn't even occur to them to worry about something that obvious. In the 2002 elections, terrorism and the fear of terrorism and the war on terrorism were like breathing—omnipresent, all-important, so obvious no one even thought to make a particularly pressing point of it.

Something was going on in the minds and souls of those Washington politicians who thought they could change the subject so quickly away from the war on terror. It was as though talking about prescription drugs, or education, or corporate scandals would indicate that the horror of the months following 9/11 was already becoming nothing more than a bad dream. A world in which prescription drugs mattered most would be a world back to normal, in which the old rules of life and politics still applied. It would not be the post-9/11 world, in which an airplane possibly aimed at the Capitol crashed instead in a Pennsylvania field; in which the Hart Senate Office Building had to be closed for six months because some malefactor sent weaponized anthrax to then Senate Majority Leader Tom Daschle; in which Georgetown hardware stores could not keep supplies of duct tape and plastic sheeting in stock. If only America's politicians could get back to doing what they already knew how to do—preen and pose and send pork back home and express fake outrage and jostle for TV time.

How do you handle a world-changing event like 9/11 when you don't like the way the world has changed? You handle it the way Democratic politicians and others on the Left handled it. You act like an ostrich. You try to get back to the way things used to be, even if there is no way back.

Now, there's no disputing that preattack topics like prescription drugs will remain political footballs, even now kicked around by parties and candidates to demonstrate to ordinary people that they "care." But in the grand scheme of things, they really don't matter a whit.

Oh, the fights are passionate. This prescription-drug plan is horrible—or it's wonderful. That school-reform plan doesn't have enough about school choice in it—or it's just great. But at a time when every sensible person in this country understands that we are in the crosshairs of mass murderers, only the blind and the desperate and the parochial could think of these matters, and Medicare reform to boot, as being of world-altering significance.

And yes, the pols will keep on blathering about them, Bush no less than the Democrats who oppose him. Both parties will continue to propose measures to solve these problems—good reforms, wasteful programs, putative fixes that themselves will have to be fixed in years to come. However, these things are simply not central to the future of a country that may literally have no future if the war on terror is mishandled. Nor are they central to this presidency.

Throughout his tenure, Bush has made dutiful and relentless use of his public appearances to promote all aspects of his agenda, from the environment to energy policy—thereby demonstrating that he has a plan for every problem and a possible answer to every question, as presidents always must if they are to seem caring and in command. Bush believes in what he says. He believes in his No Child Left Behind Act and his Clear Skies Initiative.[1] But by traveling the country and talking about matters that are really no longer central to the concerns of the American electorate, Bush is not really trying to convey the message that he has dedicated his administration to make sure an eight-year-old can read *Harry Potter and the Sorcerer's Stone.*

What he's really doing is what's known in the political-consultant trade as "inoculation." Bush continues to address most of these things to muddy efforts to criticize him, and to refute the tiresome charge that he doesn't care about the problems of ordinary people. This is the demand made on American politicians by the mushy, goody-goody, help-me-help-me, whiny aspect of contemporary American life, according to which the possibility that your child might hit his head on a playground swing and get a boo-boo is worth a prime-time special called "Are Our Children Safe?"

At the end of the Cold War, with a genuine world-ending threat suddenly gone from the earth, the very real anxieties of the nuclear age didn't just vanish. Instead, they attached themselves to concerns about which people once took a far more judicious and restrained stance. Voters had understood that Washington politicians were grappling with life-and-death issues and turned to their local politicians to deal with matters relating to the day-to-day troubles of their family life. That changed in the 1990s. Presidents were now expected to "feel your pain" and to ameliorate it. Even after September 11, George W. Bush must continue to inoculate himself by feeling our pain and sharing our anxieties.

Nevertheless, we know he's not going to sleep at night worrying about reading scores. We know his presidency is dedicated to something deeper and higher and more terrifying and more central to the future of America than childhood literacy. He knows, as we all do when we're not obsessing over our own little interests of the day, that the Bush presidency will be judged by one standard and one standard only: its response to the September 11 attacks.

And in that regard, Bush has not been like his Democratic rivals, or his Republican carpers, or those in the media inclined to second-guess him. He was not and is not an ostrich. He did not rise from that chair in the Emma E. Booker Elementary School and try to figure out what he had to do to get back to his comforting and comfortable reliance on topics like childhood literacy.

He knew that he was being challenged as few presidents had ever been challenged, and that he had a gigantic task ahead of him. He knew things would never be the same. He knew immediately that he had to change, and America had to change, and the world had to change, if America were to survive and thrive. He accepted the challenge. The deadly seriousness of the attacks and the new type of threat they represented against the citizenry of the United States required a profoundly serious response on the part of the president.

Yet it was far from assured, based on his approach to foreign and defense policy in his election campaign and during the early months of his presidency, that Bush would have a profoundly serious response to offer.

★

Candidate Bush's attitude toward American security and foreign policy had been a bit hard to decipher during his presidential campaign. He spoke in hard-line terms at times, as someone who believed American power should not be husbanded but expended to enhance American security. At other times, he was a soft-pedaler who expressed vague disapproval of the Clinton administration's use of the American military.

He talked about Clinton as though Clinton were too much of a hawk for him—as though Clinton were too adventurous militarily. But he also attacked Clinton from the Right on military matters. He spoke frequently about the need to build up the U.S. armed forces and commit more money to defense spending. He warned of a "readiness crisis" that had been created by the fact that Bill Clinton made freewheeling use of American military power without spending the funds necessary to replenish the equipment he was wearing out. Bush discussed the need to take better care of military families.

However, when President Bush released the details of his first proposed national budget a few weeks before September 11, he had only increased defense spending by a token amount. The administration's fear of creating new deficits and the cost of its tax cut had led to a clear short-changing of defense needs. Had Bush's tough talk on the military merely been a campaign weapon, a standard Republican salvo to remind the public that Democrats were not to be trusted when it came to matters of war and peace?

So disappointing was the 2002 budget to the neoconservatives at the *Weekly Standard,* the magazine that would soon be accused of hypnotizing the president into the Iraq war, that its editor William Kristol and its chief foreign-policy writer Robert Kagan wrote this coruscating paragraph in July 2001: "Here's some un-solicited advice for two old friends, Donald Rumsfeld and Paul Wolfowitz: Resign. Right now that may be the best service they could perform for their country, for it may be the only way to focus the attention of the American people—and the Bush ad-ministration—on the impending evisceration of the American military."

These words now vie with F. Scott Fitzgerald's oft-quoted re-mark about there being "no second acts in American lives" for pride of place in the Hall of Fame dedicated to Catchy But To-tally Wrong Assertions.[2] Still, Kristol and Kagan wrote them be-cause they perceived a truth about pre-9/11 Bush on defense matters: The new president wasn't quite sure where to plant his flag. Would he hew to the robust and somewhat confrontational ideological style of the Reagan administration, which believed that it was an American mission to fight tyranny and promote de-mocracy? Or would his foreign and defense policy more closely resemble the more traditional realpolitik views of his father's administration, consumed as it was with the notion of "world order"?

Nobody could really be sure. His foreign and defense policy teams were amalgams of Reaganites and Bushies, so there were few clues to be gleaned there. And candidate Dubya's only truly notable remark on the subject had come during a debate with Al Gore, when he accused the Clinton administration of a lack of humility in foreign policy. "We've got to be humble and yet project strength in a way that promotes freedom," Bush said in one of his debates with Gore. The term "humble" was again code. Bush was saying he was not interested in pursuing an adventurous foreign policy, didn't want to stick America's nose in things where it didn't belong.

Well, he broke his word. He violated a campaign promise. And thank God for it.

Bush probably owes Gore and Clinton an apology for his criticism. All of Clinton's foreign policy successes came when he pursued the more robust, Reagan-style effort to exert American power on behalf of democracy and freedom—in Haiti and Bosnia and Kosovo. Indeed, the country would have been better off if Clinton and Gore had been far less humble and far more sweeping in their assertion of American power—if they had seen that the 1993 attack on the World Trade Center, the 1998 attacks on U.S. embassies in Africa, and the 2000 attack on the USS *Cole* were the initial shots in the war on terror that escalated into unprecedented carnage on September 11.

Clinton and Gore had refused to recognize the change in the status quo those nascent acts of mass terror represented. Bush had had no choice but to recognize it. We all had to. So did the world. Bush called it "the new reality." It had just killed thousands in

New York, at the Pentagon, and in a Pennsylvania field. Live on television. But what were parameters of the new reality? Was the problem primarily the monstrous organization called Al-Qaeda, which was making trouble for the United States with no clear purpose other than to maim and murder?

That was the first and most obvious reading. A cynical political consultant would have looked at September 11 and offered this advice: Bomb Al-Qaeda, declare victory, and go on about your business. Indeed, that's what Clinton had done in 1998 after two U.S. embassies were blown up in Africa. He fired a missile at an already deserted Al-Qaeda training camp in Afghanistan and at a pharmaceutical plant in the Sudan that was supposedly manufacturing biological weapons for Osama Bin Laden. Clinton had scored a mild political success with his 1998 strikes, even though they proved to be ineffectual. Had Bush worked out some quick and dirty response to September 11, that, too, would have been greeted with general murmurs of support and some enthusiasm from an American public eager for a quick response.

But just as the Clinton ripostes in 1998 only emboldened Bin Laden and Al-Qaeda—because they led Bin Laden to believe the United States would never really come after him with all guns blazing—a quick-and-dirty Bush response in 2001 would have been a world-historical disaster. It would have emboldened Bin Laden still further, because it would have suggested to the terrorists that the United States hadn't grasped the new reality.

The thing was, the new reality wasn't merely defined by an increasingly tough, clever, and murderous Al-Qaeda. Rather, September 11 revealed that in the brave new world of the third millennium, the United States was uniquely and terrifyingly vulnerable to mass murder. Indeed, it suddenly seemed as though the United States was about as vulnerable a place as any there could be on this earth. With our expansive borders and the simple fact that 500 million—one half of one billion—human beings transit in and out of the United States every year, how could the American homeland ever again be truly secure following the revelation that our own domestic aircraft could be used as weaponry against us? With our Constitution designed to prevent the government from achieving coercive dominion over citizens and visitors alike, there was no way to lock down the United States in the wake of the attacks.

Here is what Bush understood: We are vulnerable because we are free. We are vulnerable because we are a beacon of freedom that draws hundreds of millions to bask in liberty's light, even if only for a brief moment. That beacon also provided the perfect guiding light for a team of suicide terrorists with a clever and unpredictable plan.

The nature of suicide terrorism is this: If a person makes the unfathomable decision to turn himself into a weapon, and then he succeeds in reaching his target, the question is not whether he will do damage but how much damage will he be able to do. On September 11, Al-Qaeda enlarged the capacity of suicide terrorism. Previously, such terrorism had expressed itself in monstrous but small-scale ways—individuals blowing themselves up in marketplaces or driving explosive-laden trucks into buildings. Never before had a group of suicide terrorists working in tandem succeeded in transforming airplanes into missiles for the purpose of murdering tens of thousands in terrifying synchronization. Airplanes turned into weapons of mass destruction, in other words. An individual with a Semtex-filled vest may harm one hundred people in Israel. A car bomber in Lebanon killed 241 marines in

1983. A couple of synchronized car bombs in Tanzania and Kenya in 1998 killed and injured 350. Such events were and are dreadful, disgusting, evil. But they do not have the power to rock a society to its foundations. A crew of people hijacking four planes *did* rock a society and the world. They killed three thousand; they might just as easily have killed thirty thousand if they'd managed to wait an hour before crashing their planes into the Twin Towers.

This had never happened before. Not in this way, and certainly not to us. And the domestic-airplane attack can never happen again, not in the same way, as its designers surely understood. It was a one-time shot—because once the world knows such a dastardly scheme can become reality, we can take steps to prevent something like it from ever happening again (as we have). The four-plane gambit had been used, and could not be used a second time.

Just because the means had to change didn't mean the intent couldn't remain the same, however. The intent is to kill on an unimaginable scale, to tear at the heart of this country, to cripple us emotionally and scar us psychically in ways from which we could never recover. If that is your goal, it doesn't take you long to connect the dots. What if that goal—to kill on an unimaginable scale—would best be accomplished by using not nineteen people, but a single person? After all, a lone terrorist need rely only on himself, and can move around more easily than if he were part of a crew. A lone terrorist, once inside our borders, is very nearly impossible to detect among 291 million. But can he do more damage than those nineteen?

He can—if he uses a weapon different from the Semtex vests favored by Palestinian terrorists in Israel. He can—if he is carrying a suitcase with a small nuclear device smuggled into the country in a ship container. How could that suitcase ever be properly detected? After all, 12 million—12 million!—shipping containers enter the United States every year. Or maybe he's got a vial with botulinum toxin that has been brought into the United States in a diplomatic pouch to an embassy or a U.N. mission (diplomatic pouches cannot legally be searched when they enter this country).

Our lone terrorist reaches Times Square. Or Capitol Hill. Or Disney World. Or the Mall of America. And there, pumped full of Ecstasy—which they give to Palestinian suicide bombers to make their last hours more pleasant and less stressful—the evil-doer drops the vial, or presses a makeshift button on the suitcase. Thus does a single person become a nuclear bomb. A single person becomes the delivery system for a chemical weapon. The result is the deaths of thousands, or hundreds of thousands, or millions. As Bush put it in his 2003 State of the Union address: "Chemical agents, lethal viruses, and shadowy terrorist networks are not easily contained. Imagine those nineteen hijackers with other weapons . . . it would take one vial, one canister, one crate slipped into this country to bring a day of horror like none we have ever known."

A once-legendary political scientist named Herman Kahn wrote a controversial book in 1962 about nuclear war, called *Thinking About the Unthinkable.* For attempting to imagine what the world would be like as a result of nuclear exchanges, Kahn was excoriated by the head-in-the-sand intellectuals of his time who were so petrified by the prospect that they thought it would be better just to look away.

As he stood with his foot planted on that "Y" on the rug on that classroom floor in Florida on September 11, George W. Bush did what the intellectuals of the 1960s thought was just too dangerous for a president to do. He thought about the unthinkable.

And he has not, for a moment, stopped thinking about it.

★

"One of my jobs," Bush said in November 2002, "is to remind people of the stark realities that we face. See, every morning I go into that great Oval Office and read [about] threats to our country—every morning. As a matter of fact, there hadn't [been] a morning that hadn't gone by that I haven't saw—seen or read threats. Some of them are blowhards, but we take every one of them seriously. It's the new reality."

Bush could not allow himself the luxury of dwelling on the brilliantly twisted logistics of Al-Qaeda's crime, or of dismissing those threatening the United States as "blowhards." He could not allow the perverse genius of this unthinkable series of events to limit his thinking about what other unthinkable events might follow from it.

George W. Bush understood that he was dealing with a new reality in which he might find himself forced to preside over the spiritual destruction of the United States. The extremist craving for killing American civilians might conceivably find its expression in the successful use of weapons of mass destruction against us on our own soil. There were at least several thousand people in the world who felt this craving strongly enough to flock to Al-Qaeda in hopes of satisfying it. That was horrible enough. But here's what was worse: There were at least three countries in the world with weapons of mass destruction—Iraq, Iran, and North Korea—who could not be trusted not to use them whenever they decided it would be in their interest to do so. Because of the shifting nature of geopolitics following the collapse of the Soviet Union, there was little to stop them if they chose to act in a dastardly fashion.

Look at it this way, and there are only two pathways into the future.

Pathway #1: The United States goes into a state of lockdown. To defend ourselves from the possibility of attack, the entire country reconciles itself to living in constant readiness. Every package is searched. Every journey through the airport takes three hours. Every building, every facility, everywhere is guarded and hardened. We shut ourselves up tight.

Pathway #2: We change the conditions outside the United States that have led us to this pass. In other words, we change the world to save ourselves.

Bush has rejected Pathway #1 and chosen Pathway #2 instead. He refuses to accede to the permanent disruption of American commerce with all the attendant costs in the form of unemployment and slow economic growth and inflation. That sort of capitulation to terrorism would only hasten the conversion of this country into the United Gates of America. The country envisioned by those who complain Bush has not done enough to secure the homeland is a nation turned in upon itself—in which the federal government attempts to cosset Americans in a blanket of regulatory security that could never possibly be large enough to make Americans secure.

It's one thing to take prudent steps to protect ourselves. It's quite another to change American society from the ground up as a result, to live in a defensive crouch. We should not suffer economic hardship, and job loss, and punitive regulation as a direct result of being assaulted for the crime of being the richest and freest nation in the world. We should not live in homes that have windows sealed with duct tape and plastic sheeting in perpetuity. We should not have to build a fortress and then hide inside it.

Choosing to do so would, in essence, punish the innocent and reward the guilty.

It should not be necessary for ordinary American life to change. But how could we ensure that we take Pathway #2 to a more secure future without being consigned to duct-taped fear? The answer: The new reality created by September 11 could not stand. The lives of terrorists and their supporters would have to change. We would, Bush said, "smoke them out of their holes," send them running, defund them, destroy them.

The new reality was characterized by Al-Qaeda plotting against America. But that was only the very tip of the iceberg. If you went a little deeper, you could see that the new reality was defined as well by the Taliban regime in Afghanistan, which was protecting and supporting Al-Qaeda and Osama Bin Laden. Go deeper still: The new reality was supported by a lax international financial and political system that was being played brilliantly by Al-Qaeda to shield itself and its assets from detection.

This part of George W. Bush's vision was pretty uncontroversial. And it was unquestionably George W. Bush's vision. It was his decision to revise his September 12 speech to broaden the war on terrorism out from the perpetrators of September 11 to their accomplices. He defined terrorism in an expansive way by including "those who harbor" terrorist groups as well as the terrorist groups themselves. His stance received nearly unanimous support from American and European politicians and the sympathy of much of the world. Few could deny the outrage that had been inflicted on the United States, and the necessity to respond. Much of the world united behind these principles: Al-Qaeda had to go, and so did the Taliban, and so, too, did the financial networks that connected them.

A month after September 11, the United States went to war

in Afghanistan—a war unlike any that had ever been fought. A combination of American Special Forces, American air power, and Afghans on the ground took out the Taliban and routed Al-Qaeda at a cost of astonishingly few American or Afghan lives. The mission was not a perfect success, by any means. Osama Bin Laden slipped through our fingers, and we made the crucial mistake of refusing to hunt him down through the caves of Tora Bora and destroy Al-Qaeda operatives one by one.

Still, the victory was awe-inspiring—conducted with a pinpoint accuracy never before seen in history. A regime had been ended and a new one installed in the most advanced way. The method of victory was a tribute to the brilliance of the U.S. armed forces, and it was a message to tyrants and lunatics around the world: *Go after us and we can take you out without much fuss.*

But Bush was unwilling to leave it there. It would not be enough to make war on Al-Qaeda, or on their partners and enablers, the Taliban. The new reality would not be upended merely by besting them and interrupting their finances. Terrorism was a hydra-headed beast. If you succeeded in cutting its head off in Afghanistan, it would grow dozens of others—in Lebanon, in the Philippines, in Malaysia, and who knows where else. George W. Bush would have to declare war on the new reality as a whole. The only way to protect America was to change the world.

There was, in this new millennium, no brake on the ambitions of our enemies other than the threat of U.S. military action. There were no intermediaries we could use, no Soviet Union to tell Iraq or Syria or North Korea on the q.t. to cool it because the Russians didn't want to ignite a worldwide cataclysm. There was no force to oppose the bad guys except that of the United States. We were the only possible brake on their ambitions.

Over the months that passed after September 11, Bush made

it clear that the way to deal with the threat posed by terrorists was to think about the unthinkable and plan as though the terrorists were planning to unleash the ultimate weaponry against us. "We'll be deliberate, yet time is not on our side," Bush said in January 2002. "I will not wait on events while dangers gather. I will not stand by as peril draws closer and closer. The United States of America will not permit the world's most dangerous regimes to threaten us with the world's most destructive weapons."

He was about to take his next visionary step—and the uncontroversial war on terror was about to become far more controversial and far more critical.

Crazy Liberal Idea #7

Bush Is a Cowboy

George W. Bush is often dismissed for supposedly possessing a "black-and-white" view of morality (though you would think in these politically correct days this figure of speech would have long since been retired). Such a clear-cut moral perspective is considered simplistic in many quarters. The very same people who criticize Bush for this perspective amuse themselves by referring to him constantly as a "cowboy"—which is itself surely the most simplistic rendering of American foreign-policy leadership since the days of Ronald Reagan.

Reagan was also called a "cowboy" because he liked to ride horses on his California ranch and believed that the Soviet Union and other Communist countries should be confronted rather than appeased. Bush, too, owns a ranch, and he believes that terrorists and the nations that harbor and sponsor them should not be appeased. Therefore, he, too, is a "cowboy."

This is not only a caricature; it's not even the *right* caricature.

Reagan and Bush are ranchers, not cowboys. The "cowboy" of Hollywood legend was a free-ranging fellow who never settled down. The cowboy didn't *own* a ranch. More often than not, the cowboy was forced into a showdown with an evil rancher. But when you're busy reducing the most vital issues in the world to the crassest of cartoons, why even seek to render them with any verisimilitude?

Maureen Dowd of the *New York Times* is especially obsessed with the "cowboy" thing. She seems practically unable to write about Bush without making derisive use of the "c" word. George W. Bush, she has written, is "ferocious, spitting cowboy threats."[1] She has described Bush as "the gun-toting, tough-talking cowboy in the White House . . . the cowboy in the Oval Office who likes to brag of America as 'the greatest nation on the face of the Earth.' "[2] (Shame on Bush for believing and saying something so . . . so . . . so, well, so *true*.) After the Republican victories in the 2002 midterm elections, Bush was "a suddenly unstoppable cowboy." Then, in a bizarre column likening Bush to *Vogue* editor Anna Wintour, Dowd downgraded him a bit to "the cocky, laid-back Texan in cowboy boots who dictates how we live." But soon enough, the president was upgraded again from boots-wearer alone into full regalia. He was "the cowboy in chief [with] his shoot-'em-up-now-and-check-for-weapons-later posse."[3] On March 9, 2003, in honor of the upcoming war with Iraq, Dowd dubbed Bush the "Xanax Cowboy,"[4] because he displayed a grim and sober visage during a press conference.

Xanax is an antianxiety medication, and Dowd's use of the term suggests she is suffering from what psychiatrists call "projection." Given the thinly disguised hysteria with which she greeted each hint of a possible chemical or biological attack after September 11, Dowd herself made it sound in her own column as though she needed some Xanax pretty badly. She confessed in an October 2001 piece that she had taken to writing her columns with protective gloves on her hands for fear of anthrax contamination.

Dowd appears to have chosen to focus her alarm on Bush rather than on anthrax. "It's really scary to think," she shuddered, "that we are even scaring Russia and China." Given the alarming degree of fretting she has done over the past few years, Xanax really might not be the right drug for Dowd. Its antianxiety effects only last a few hours. Perhaps a career change might help.

Dowd may be the worst, or the silliest, of the cowboy-punchers, but she certainly isn't the only one. A search of the Nexis database from 2001 through 2003 reveals the term "cowboy" used in the media in conjunction with Bush's name at least three thousand times—and it's highly doubtful that the conjunction has ever been made in a manner friendly to Bush. The Nexis database doesn't include French or German or most other European media outlets, where the comparison of George W. Bush to a cowboy is used even more obsessively than in a Maureen Dowd column.

The reason for the resuscitation of the Reagan caricature, of course, is that George W. Bush has pursued a foreign policy detested by those who draw the caricature. They believe that, like the cowboy of legend, Bush *wants* to go it alone and to do so with guns blazing: "Too often, this administration has given, to many Americans and even more to foreigners, the impression that it is drunk with power, that it has somehow absorbed the . . . spirit of the Athenian generals who, Thucydides tells us, informed the Melians that, between the strong and the weak, only the language of power matters."[5]

Thus spake Stanley Hoffman of Harvard University, writing

in the *New York Review of Books*. Hoffman uses the Melian debate as a sotto-voce message to those who remember their college Thucydides. At the end of the debate about the sovereignty of the island of Melos in *The Peloponnesian War*, Thucydides writes, the Athenians "put to death all who were of military age, and made slaves of the women and children. They then colonized the island, sending thither five hundred settlers of their own. . . ."[6] With what passes for subtlety, Stanley Hoffman is suggesting that the end result of our involvement in Iraq might be that the United States will decide to commit mass murder and colonize the country.

Hoffman has it exactly backwards, of course, as what happened in Iraq was the country's liberation from a mass murderer named Saddam Hussein who had taken the place over in 1969. But then, Stanley Hoffman's august standing as a foreign-policy critic is belied by the fact that he has, over the past forty years, been demonstrably wrong about very nearly everything when it comes to American foreign policy. If he had been in charge of the State Department since the days of the Vietnam War and his proposals and recommendations followed to the letter, I believe the following would be true today: The Soviet Union would still be standing, with Afghanistan firmly in its pocket; democratic Taiwan would have been swallowed up by Communist China; Cuba would have been unchecked in its efforts to spread revolution throughout Central and South America; and Israel would be fighting for its life behind unsustainable borders. So you might want to take what he says with just the tiniest grain of salt.

Hoffman is comparing this moment in American history to the moment when (in Thucydides's eyes) Athens began to lose its soul. The editorialists of the *New York Times* have taken a similarly grand historical tack by comparing the Bush administration's national-security strategy to "a pronouncement that the Roman Empire or Napoleon might have produced."[7] This is an appalling thing to say, especially considering that the national security document the *Times* was criticizing is notable for the ennobling prescription it offers for an end to world chaos: Democracy in the American vein. Such a liberal, life-enhancing outcome was hardly the goal of the Roman Empire or Napoleon. Indeed, in the same editorial, the *Times* acknowledged some sections of the national-security document were "animated by the most enlightened and constructive principles of the land of Jefferson, Lincoln and the Marshall Plan."

There is a massive illogic here, and it's not the Bush administration's. A nation *can't* simultaneously emulate the Roman Empire and execute the Marshall Plan. You can't be Napoleon and Jefferson at the same time. America—let me say it loud enough so it can be heard in the cheap seats—is not attempting to dominate. It is seeking to liberate.

"Mr. Bush," the *Times* concluded, "must be careful not to create a Fortress America." In yet another example of the *Times's* rhetorical dishonesty (or, perhaps, illiteracy), the editorialists are twisting accepted foreign-policy language for their own deceptive purposes. The term "Fortress America" has been used for decades as a warning of what will happen if the United States goes isolationist—if it places itself in an entirely defensive posture and loses interest in the rest of the world. George W. Bush has *engaged* the United States with the rest of the world in a very direct way. Indeed, he has explicitly stated that any fantasies of a "Fortress America" have been rendered moot by the rise of international terrorism. "Oceans that separated us from other continents no longer separate us from dangers," he said on November 27, 2002, as he signed the legislation creating the Department of Homeland Security.

The same corruption of terminology can be seen in a number of far-Left critiques of Bush's foreign policy. In the essay collection *Power Shift: U.S. Unilateralism and Global Strategy After September 11,* the leftist journalist Tom Barry writes slightingly of the "America First convictions of the Bush supremacists."[8] "America First" was the isolationist slogan used by Henry Ford, Charles Lindbergh, and others during their effort to keep the United States out of World War II. "America First" cannot properly be used to describe an administration that has undertaken a massive effort to change the Middle East and the world for the better, especially since many America Firsters of the 1930s were also Nazi sympathizers.

You don't have to be a committed Left-wing activist like Barry, though, to declare that our "cowboy" president is a dangerous go-it-alone unilateralist. The word "unilateralist" has been attached to Bush's foreign policy with Krazy Glue by every American journalist who has taken a trip abroad and is cornered by an angry European.

As we have seen, Bush was open and honest in 2001 about the fact that the United States would never ratify the Kyoto environmental treaty—a matter that had been settled long before he ever took office. That same year he told Vladimir Putin and Russia the truth about an anti-ballistic missile treaty that was harmful and obsolete. But in the view of Fareed Zakaria, the *Newsweek* columnist who occupies a position about as middle-of-the-road as a painted yellow line, "In its first year the administration withdrew from five international treaties—and did so as brusquely as it could. . . . It developed a language and diplomatic style that seemed calculated to offend the world."[9] In other words, what really enraged self-appointed foreign-policy wise men here and abroad was that Bush had quashed their ability to live a fantasy—a fantasy in which the world's only superpower would be willing and eager to have its decisions vetted and even vetoed on the grounds that they might offend someone, somewhere.

Bush has also repeatedly been accused of "defying" the international community. Under normal conditions, one friend wouldn't accuse another friend who disagrees with him of "defiance." But the mandarins of Western Europe have decided Bush is not their friend. And then, having shown uncommon arrogance by condemning Bush's "defiance"—as though he and the United States are not permitted, somehow, to reach conclusions that differ from theirs—they have continued to turn back and hurl the charge of "arrogance" at Bush himself.

The truth is there was no condescension or arrogance in Bush's conclusions. He treated the nations supporting the Kyoto treaty and the government of Russia with the respect any adult owes another adult: He was straight with them. He refused to bow to pretense. He did not play games or pursue fictions. All that this has done is made him vulnerable to some pretty foul game-playing on the part of those who complain that he is both arrogant and a "cowboy." Bush spent seven months, from September 2002 to March 2003, in intense diplomatic efforts to convince the Security Council of the United Nations to be a full partner in the effort to enforce its own sixteen resolutions that had to do with Iraq. Many Americans, indeed many in his own administration, considered his efforts at the United Nations a waste of time and the act of courting the Security Council a potential national humiliation. Bush did not. Indeed, the "go-it-alone" cowboy knew that his dedicated ally, British Prime Minister Tony Blair, believed ardently in the need for the U.N.'s support, and Bush did what he could to reward Blair's steadfastness. Bush and Blair succeeded in getting the resolution they needed, Resolution 1441, with its language calling for "serious consequences" if Saddam Hussein did not comply with the demands of U.N. weapons inspectors. Saddam did not. Still, Blair and others were so insistent on receiving a thoroughgoing mandate from the United Nations that Bush agreed to go back to the United Nations a second time. The "cowboy and his posse" then spent weeks trying to secure the support of nations like Guinea and Uganda, which is really not something a cowboy out of a Hollywood movie would usually put himself out to do. Democrats running against him for president have since had the colossal gall to blame Bush for "failing" to secure United Nations participation in the Iraq war—as though he had not done everything he could to do just that short of saying he would not fight the war.

Bush has received no credit for his indefatigable efforts at diplomacy in the buildup to the war in Iraq, either at the United Nations or in the assembly of a thirty-three-nation "coalition of the willing." That coalition has usually been dismissed with a strange and offensive contempt, as though any country that would back someone like Bush was by definition a penny-ante place. It meant nothing to Bush's critics, because when they talk about how important it was for Bush to secure "diplomatic support," they're actually lying. The only support they cared about would have come from Russia, France, and Germany—probably because they knew it was the support he would never, ever get. Even Democrats who voted to support the war in Iraq have taken to making wild claims about the vital importance of Russia, France, and Germany. As Congressman Dick Gephardt put it in an October 2003 Democratic presidential debate: "Bush keeps saying we've got thirty countries helping us. Yes, Togo sent one soldier. That isn't what we need. We need France, Germany, Russia. There's only three countries in the world that can give us both the financial and the military help that we need."

Only three countries? It's rude but understandable that Gephardt would dismiss Togo. But what about Japan? Italy? Britain? Spain? Australia? Does the stalwart support for the war in Iraq and the stalwart help afterward from these wealthy, first-world nations mean nothing? Of course not. It means a great deal. But for those who look for every opportunity to criticize George Bush for being a cowboy, facts can't be permitted to intrude on their preposterous fantasies.

8

The Visionary

In the aftermath of the war on Al-Qaeda and the Taliban, Bush continued to accept the responsibility for "thinking about the unthinkable"—and about preventing the threat from the world's most dangerous regimes. And at the beginning of June 2002, he announced that the new reality required a new American doctrine to challenge it.

In a speech delivered at the commencement ceremonies for the United States Military Academy at West Point, Bush made the stunning announcement that the two pillars of American foreign policy had become outdated: "America's defense relied on the Cold War doctrines of deterrence and containment. In some cases, those strategies still apply. But new threats also require new thinking."

Deterrence, Bush explained, was "the promise of massive retaliation against nations." The policy had worked to keep the world from exploding into nuclear war for fifty years. But deterrence was not an effective strategy, Bush said, "against shadowy terrorist networks with no nation or citizens to defend." As for containment, it was the name given to the policy the United States used to oppose the spread of Communism to countries other than the Soviet Union and its satellites in Eastern Europe. It, too, was brilliantly successful and helped lead eventually to the destruction of Soviet communism. But, Bush said, containment "is not possible when unbalanced dictators with weapons of mass destruction can deliver those weapons on missiles or secretly provide them to terrorist allies."

If deterrence and containment no longer work, then what? In a word: Preemption. Bush declared that the United States would now hew to a doctrine that permitted us to attack a rogue nation if we believed that nation would soon pose a terrible danger. "We cannot defend America and our friends by hoping for the best," he said. "We cannot put our faith in the word of tyrants, who solemnly sign nonproliferation treaties, and then systematically break them. If we wait for threats to fully materialize, we will have waited too long."

Those words are at the heart of the argument for the American war with Iraq in 2003. There were many other arguments advanced by the administration as well for that war, and they were all formidable: Iraq's continued defiance of U.N. resolutions to which it had agreed, its flouting of international law, the virtue and value of ridding the world of a monstrous tyrant. But the war was about the Iraqi threat—or, more precisely, the inevitability of an Iraqi threat in the near future. In the view of the new Bush doctrine, the threat did not need to be immediate, actually *should not be immediate,* because "if we wait for threats to fully materialize, we will have waited too long." If the United

States judged that Saddam Hussein were to pose a danger in the near future, that would be more than reason enough to take him out now—because what he would threaten us with would be weaponry of mass destruction, against which, if he combined them with a suicide terrorist, there is little or no defense.

We knew Saddam had had no compunction about using chemical and biological agents against his own people, with a death and casualty toll in the tens of thousands. He was months away from a nuclear bomb when the Israelis blew up the Osirak reactor in 1981, and we discovered following the Persian Gulf War he had been a year away from a bomb in 1991. Given the rise in suicide terrorism and the proven capacity of a single suicide terrorist to deliver a weapon of mass destruction in exchange for a promise of seventy-two black-eyed virgins in heaven, Saddam was now more potentially dangerous to the United States than he ever had been. He had become a hero to suicide bombers because he was paying out $25,000 cash bonuses to the families of those Palestinian "martyrs" who blew up Israelis as they blew themselves up. In a world with suicide terrorists, rogue nations, and weapons of mass destruction, there is no margin for error. One slipup and millions will die in New York. "No margin for error" is a phrase Bush used dozens of times in the aftermath of the September 11 attacks.

In fact, since the Saddam threat had not yet fully coalesced, Bush believed we had been presented with a tactical advantage we did not possess when it came to a nation like North Korea. The insane Pyongyang regime had informed us in the summer of 2001 that it was ready to bring a nuclear plant online to manufacture bombs, and that nothing we could do or say would stop it. Here was a perfectly realized example of how we had "waited too long."

Because a threat had *fully* materialized in North Korea, our options were pitifully narrow. The president never, never once, said that Saddam Hussein was in a position to kill us all in the months surrounding the war in Iraq.[1] What he did say—what the 2002 National Intelligence Estimate, a classified document representing the consensus view of U.S. intelligence agencies, said when it was delivered to him in 2002—was that Saddam could have a nuclear weapon by 2006. Bush looked into that possible future, that 2006, and didn't like what he saw. He had to prevent it. And he did.

The world will never know what kind of threat Saddam Hussein might have posed with a fully reconstituted weapons-of-mass-destruction program. The world will never know because Bush "adopted a new strategy for a new kind of war," as he told a crowd in St. Louis in August 2003. "We will not wait for known enemies to strike us again. We will strike them and their camps or caves or wherever they hide before they hit more of our cities and kill more of our citizens. We will do everything in our power to deny terrorists weapons of mass destruction before they can commit murder on an unimaginable scale."

That is the gift George W. Bush has given to the world—even though so many of his own craven countrymen among the liberal elites, so eager to believe the worst of him, will not accept it and insist on believing it poisoned. In Iraq, as it had in Afghanistan, the U.S. military removed a dreadful regime from power with staggering precision and a heartening lack of bloodshed. As Bush explained on May 1, 2003: "With new tactics and precision weapons, we can achieve military objectives without directing violence against civilians. No device of man can remove the tragedy from war; yet it is a great moral advance when the guilty have far more to fear from war than the innocent." This genuine moral advance in the conduct of war is taken entirely for granted by Bush's critics. They express no sense of relief that our 150,000 troops were so little bloodied, or that Iraqis got through the war so quickly and painlessly that some of them had the luxury of quickly complaining they didn't have sufficient creature comforts in its aftermath.

★

The new reality was being supported by Europeans who have chosen to give sympathetic hearings to terrorist groups, Palestinian groups especially. Their sympathy was in part due to misguided humanitarianism and in part to cynical power concerns. With burgeoning Muslim immigrant populations, nations like France and Germany had reason to think they could buy civil peace by aggressively criticizing Israel and offering rhetorical aid and comfort to terrorists who attacked innocent Israeli civilians. That kind of sympathy could no longer be acceptable as a part of international foreign policy, in Bush's view. All a lone terrorist who might otherwise blow up a Jerusalem bus would need is a plane ticket supplied by a friendly European and a handler here in the States and he could be in Times Square with an envelope filled with weapons-grade anthrax. Bush challenged the Europeans to treat other groups—Hamas and Islamic Jihad and Hezbollah, the vicious shock troops of Jew-killing Palestinian radicalism—as they had agreed to treat Al-Qaeda.

This is the point at which things began to get sticky for Bush and the United States with so many of the nations that had expressed sympathy, support, and good fellowship with America following the devastation of September 11. The world, even the anti-American leftists of Europe, had come to love us as we lay injured. A damaged America, a weakened America, a bloodied America—that was an America with which they could show solidarity.[2] But America did not remain damaged, weakened, bloodied. America proved to be, as Bush said no fewer than 150 times in the two years that followed, "strong."

Once that strength was asserted, America was not quite so lovable to its post–September 11 admirers. The resurgent America—the nation that declared worldwide war against terrorism and against rogue nations that might arm terrorists—really meant business. We did go after the Taliban, as we had said we would, for harboring Al-Qaeda. And we went after Al-Qaeda, as we had said we would. Then, following the triumph in Afghanistan, Bush turned his attention to the Palestinians and Iraq. And it was with George W. Bush's reaction to, relation with, and conduct toward these two entities that the truly visionary aspect of his presidency came to be revealed in its fullest flowering.

★

To discuss the Palestinian leadership and Iraq, we have to discuss the most delicate and difficult—and also the most dangerous— aspect of the new reality. And that is militant Islam.

The president genuinely believes that Islam is a religion of peace. He believes that as one of the world's three great monotheistic faiths, Islam offers a message of hope and love and salvation that may be different from the religious teachings of his own church but is equally deserving of respect. "It's really important for somebody in my position to live the Word," he told

U.S. News and World Report, "but also understand that people communicate with God and reach God in different ways. It just doesn't have to be my way. . . . I am mindful of what Billy Graham one time told me, for me not to try to figure out—try to pick and choose who gets to go to heaven."[3]

He also believes that American Muslims deserve special protection in these difficult days, and has been too little acknowledged for the determined emphasis he placed on their safety and security. In the crazy weeks after September 11, he made constant mention of them and exhorted Americans to respect them and their faith. His actions, as David Frum points out in *The Right Man,* may have saved hundreds of lives.

Still, Islam is as intricately woven into the pattern of the new reality as the colors in a Shiraz rug. The threat to the United States comes primarily from Muslims who follow, or are influenced by, one of the two major strains of militant Islam.

The first strain is the religious-extremist version peddled by Osama Bin Laden. The Muslim extremists are obsessed with the holy sites of Mecca and Medina, which are located inside the kingdom of Saudi Arabia. The Bin Ladenites consider the Saudi regime's decision to allow the United States to take a role in assuring the protection of the holy sites an unforgivable act of sacrilegious perfidy. The American role (which came about when the United States was asked by Saudi Arabia in 1990 to protect the holy sites from the marauding army of Iraq before the first Gulf War) is seen as the final humiliation in a three-century onslaught against Islam that began when the Muslim horde was expelled from Europe following their loss at the gates of Vienna— on September 11, 1683.

In its second guise, militant Islam takes a secular-nationalist

form. Its two primary adherents: Saddam Hussein and Yasser Arafat. Their desire to challenge the United States and Israel stems
not only from Islamic tradition but also the dark contemporary
ideologies of Nazism and Communism. Both -isms had a great
influence on the imagery, organizational style, and ends-justifies-
the-means politics practiced by these canny mass murderers.

Arafat's Palestinian Authority and Hussein's Iraq have arguably
been the world's two most destabilizing forces these past thirty
years or more. Arafat brought civil war to Jordan in the late
1960s. After his expulsion from Jordan in 1970, he went on to
destroy the functioning nation of Lebanon until he was finally
expelled from there in 1983. Brought back into the West Bank
in 1994 by the Oslo accords with Israel, he destroyed any chance
of a peaceful transition to a two-state solution by instigating a
second Intifada in September 2000. As for Saddam Hussein, he
effectively took power in 1969, began a ten-year war with Iran in
1979, took over Kuwait in 1990, and then spent a decade challenging the United Nations and the United States when they so
carelessly allowed him to remain in power. Like parasites and
viruses, militant Islam in its secular-nationalist guise thrives on
instability and flourishes in chaos.

Add the perpetual instability of the Arafat-Hussein axis to the
fanatical determination of the religious militants led by Osama
Bin Laden, and what do you have? You have the new reality. It
can come at you from any angle and in any way. The two strains
of militant Islam are not bound by any morality other than the
morality of their ultimate victory. And their combined destructive
potential could make September 11 look like a hootenanny.

The two strains are not identical. They have differences and
antagonisms. But neither are they enemies. They have worked
together and plotted together and played together for decades.

And they have a common enemy in us, a fact that often helps strengthen bonds of affection that might otherwise be weak.

This is a partial explanation of why George W. Bush targeted both the regime in Iraq and the Palestinian Authority for destruction and overhaul in 2002. Having taken on militant Islam in its fundamentalist guise in Afghanistan was not enough. Militant Islam also had to be taken on in its secular-nationalist form.[4] An incredibly daunting challenge, to put it mildly. Bush knows it, and he knows as well that you can't replace something—even something evil—with nothing. You can't frighten the enemy into perpetual submission, and we don't want to live in a state of perpetual war.

Bush again thought about what had previously been considered unthinkable, and he concluded that the solution to terrorism and militant Islam was nothing less than . . . freedom. Having hinted at this thought in the aftermath of the Afghan war, Bush brought it into play on June 24, 2002, when he delivered a major speech on Israel and the Palestinians that resolved two months of internecine squabbling within his administration on the subject of the Second Palestinian Intifada.

By June 24, the terrorist war staged by the Palestinians against the Israeli populace had been going on for twenty months. Palestinian suicide bombers—many of them directly connected to strongman Yasser Arafat's Fatah faction by their membership in the Al Aqsa Martyrs Brigade—had been staging deadly attacks on Israeli civilians on what at times came close to being on a daily basis. The casualty statistics were sickening: 786 dead and more than 2,000 injured in a population of 5 million. Proportionately, the terrorist toll on the Israelis was ten times greater than that of the September 11 bombings on the United States.

The Israeli government's response had been twofold. It attempted to decapitate the four key Palestinian terrorist organizations, and it decided to hold Yasser Arafat personally responsible for the killings. In March 2002, the Israeli government isolated him in his headquarters in Ramallah, would not let him leave, would not negotiate with him, and began to talk openly about expelling or killing him.

George W. Bush and the U.S. government had cut Arafat off by this time as well. Bush himself had always been ill-disposed toward Arafat, and would not meet with him. But in December 2001, Arafat made a fatal mistake: He lied unashamedly to Secretary of State Colin Powell when he claimed to have no knowledge of a weapons-laden ship called the *Karine A.*—loaded with more than fifty tons of bombs and the like—that had been captured by the Israelis in the Red Sea. Intelligence intercepts demonstrated that the ship's cargo had been sought and the plan approved by Arafat himself.

That was it for Bush. Arafat was an untouchable as far as the president was concerned. He was now, had always been, and would always be a terrorist. He was not to be considered an acceptable interlocutor. The Bush administration would have nothing more to do with Arafat. Instead, Bush said, he wanted to deal with a new Palestinian leadership.

But the president had a problem. He believed (correctly, in my view) that the Palestinians were the guilty party in the Intifada. They were attacking ordinary Israelis on buses and in marketplaces, trying to destroy a civil society from the inside, even though Israel had offered Arafat a fantastically generous deal for a state in August 2000. But European and Arab countries alike had decided that the real villains of the Intifada were the Israelis, and the State Department kept hearing incessantly from them on the matter. How, the Europeans wanted to know, could we expect Arab countries to work with us on isolating Al-Qaeda when we seemed so "one-sided" when it came to the Palestinian-Israeli war?

British Prime Minister Tony Blair, a far more persuasive European voice in the war on terror than any other, came to the United States at the beginning of April 2002 with the same message about the Israeli-Palestinian conflict. Grateful for Blair's friendship and support, Bush seemed for a time to respond. The president angrily demanded that Israel "withdraw without delay" from Palestinian areas.

Yet when Israel did what he asked, the Palestinians responded with more terror. Bush was in a quandary. He had said repeatedly that Israel had the right to defend itself against terror, just like the United States. The world—and some of those experts working for him—seemed to be of the view that the Palestinian terror attacks on innocent civilians were somehow legitimate military responses to Israeli actions.

Bush's view was consistent. The view of those who wanted to appease the Palestinian leaders was not. Nor was the view of Bush's own State Department. Word had leaked out of Foggy Bottom of a new proposal by Secretary of State Colin Powell and others to impose on Israel a specific timeline for a Palestinian state. That plan, which came to be known as the "road map," would in effect have rewarded terror by announcing the creation of a state by date certain without first requiring a cessation of the Intifada. There was also a certain amount of blithering about a phony peace plan offered by the ruler of Saudi Arabia.[5]

Finally, after bouncing back and forth, Bush stepped into the Rose Garden on June 24, 2002, and spoke his mind, his heart, his soul—and his vision.

Just as the new reality that had brought about September 11 could not stand, Bush suggested, neither could the new reality between Israel and the Palestinians. "For the sake of all humanity, things must change in the Middle East," Bush said. "It is untenable for Israeli citizens to live in terror. It is untenable for Palestinians to live in squalor and occupation. And the current situation offers no prospect that life will improve. Israeli citizens will continue to be victimized by terrorists, and so Israel will continue to defend herself." Bush's answer was for the Palestinians to oust Yasser Arafat and make room for more reasonable interlocutors with the Israelis: "I call on the Palestinian people to elect new leaders, leaders not compromised by terror."

However, new leaders would not be enough. The only real solution was something much greater, much grander: "I call upon [the Palestinians] to build a practicing democracy, based on tolerance and liberty. . . . If Palestinians embrace democracy, confront corruption, and firmly reject terror, they can count on American support for the creation of a provisional state of Palestine."

Bush argued that the rage in the Palestinian body politic was due to a lack of liberty, not a lack of statehood. "I can understand the deep anger and despair of the Palestinian people," he said in the most compassionate words ever spoken about the stateless people by an American president. "For decades you've been treated as pawns in the Middle East conflict. Your interests have been held hostage to a comprehensive peace agreement that never seems to come, as your lives get worse year by year. You deserve democracy and the rule of law. You deserve an open society and a thriving economy. You deserve a life of hope for your children. An end to occupation and a peaceful democratic Palestinian state may seem distant, but America and our partners throughout the world stand ready to help, help you make them possible as soon as possible." This vision of liberty for the Palestinians need not begin and end there: "If liberty can blossom in the rocky soil of the West Bank and Gaza, it will inspire millions of men and women around the globe who are equally weary of poverty and oppression, equally entitled to the benefits of democratic government."

Bush's notion that democratic principles should be brought to play in the Muslim world—not just lip-service democracy, like being able to cast a vote every once in a while, but the full range of freedoms and institutions that took root in the United States owing to our Declaration of Independence and our Constitution—is the truly visionary aspect of the presidency of George W. Bush.

"I have a hope for the people of Muslim countries," he said. "Your commitments to morality, and learning, and tolerance led to great historical achievements. And those values are alive in the Islamic world today. You have a rich culture, and you share the aspirations of men and women in every culture. Prosperity and freedom and dignity are not just American hopes, or Western hopes. They are universal, human hopes. And even in the violence and turmoil of the Middle East, America believes those hopes have the power to transform lives and nations."

And so Bush began in earnest a titanically ambitious project that frankly and without apology envisions a world vastly different, vastly better and vastly safer for Americans thirty years from now than the world today: "This moment is both an opportunity and a test for all parties in the Middle East: an opportunity to lay the foundations for future peace; a test to show who is serious about peace and who is not. The choice here is stark and simple. The Bible says, 'I have set before you life and death; therefore, choose life.' The time has arrived for everyone in this conflict to choose peace, and hope, and life."

★

In the minds of many sophisticates, this is a naïve, deluded vision. On the Right, there are skeptics who cannot believe American-style democracy could ever take root in the Muslim world, in part because the very structure of Islam makes the idea of a separation between church and state impossible. On the Left, there are people who believe that imposing American-style democracy on Islamic countries is an act of imperialist arrogance. After all, who are we to imagine that our way of life, which grants us freedom of speech and religion and assembly and the pursuit of happiness and a thousand other blessings, is any better than the life of a woman in a burqa leading an existence in a society that refuses to allow her to become literate and that has left her as little more than human chattel?

Foreign-policy "realists," who occupy a lofty zone beyond Left and Right, look at the history of Islamic countries and the Middle East and simply say it is utopian and unrealistic to offer American-style government as an alternative to peoples who have lived either tribally or under the strongman's yoke for 1,400 years.

Bush knows something the skeptics do not know. He knows that just as a politician must have an answer to the question "What are you doing about reading scores?" so, too, does a world leader facing a peril that could destroy his country need an answer to the question "What are you doing to make sure the peril goes away for good?" Freedom and democracy are his answers.

The promise at the beginning of the Cold War was that we could defeat our totalitarian enemy not by destroying his country and laying him to waste, but by helping the internal contradictions and evils inside his own society to cause the tyranny to crack from within. We would fight the Cold War not only to protect ourselves but, in the end, to make the world a better place. The fight was worthwhile, and the result was the eventual collapse of the Soviet Empire and the democratization of Eastern Europe.

The Bush doctrine promises a Middle East similarly altered for the better, because only if the Middle East is remade over the coming decades can the United States be truly safe.

Crazy Liberal Idea #8

Bush Is a Liar

By the advent of the autumn of 2003, it had become conventional wisdom among liberals and Democrats that George W. Bush had consciously and with malice aforethought deceived the United States and the world about the need for a war with Iraq, the reasons for it, and the grounds on which it was fought. The point was hammered home by three books published at almost exactly the same time with eerily similar titles and entirely congruent points of view—Al Franken's *Lies and the Lying Liars Who Tell Them*, David Corn's *Lies of George W. Bush*, and Joe Conason's *Big Lies*.

Lies, lies, and more lies. "The war with Iraq started with the full government standing right up and looking you in the eye and openly lying," writes the columnist Jimmy Breslin. "Can you believe anything Bush says? Only if you're a rank sucker."[1] Andrew Greeley writes, "The present administration has proven itself very skilled at spinning reality so that truth becomes invisible."[2]

Ira Chernus, professor of religious studies at the University of Colorado, has a particularly inventive explanation for Bush's untruths: "Lies had to be told because Saddam had to go—not because he was a ruthless dictator, but because he was a successful model of resisting economic globalization." Here we have Bush-hatred at its most pure, so pure that it inadvertently succeeded in turning Saddam Hussein, one of the most loathsome men who has ever walked the earth, into something of a counterculture symbol for opposing Bush and the United States.

At its most impure—which is to say, its most nakedly partisan—Bush-hatred spewed from the Rabelaisian mouth of Edward Kennedy in mid-September 2003. "This whole thing was a fraud," the Massachusetts senator frothed. "This was made up in Texas, announced in January [2003] to the Republican leadership that the war was going to take place and was going to be good politically." The retired and aggrieved Al Gore had returned to the public stage a month earlier with a roaring flourish to challenge Bush's honesty. "Robust debate in a democracy will almost always involve occasional rhetorical excesses and leaps of faith," Gore said. "But there is a big difference between that and a systematic effort to manipulate facts in service to a totalistic ideology felt to be more important than basic honesty. Unfortunately, I think it is no longer possible to avoid the conclusion that what the country is dealing with in the Bush presidency is the latter."[3]

Much of the blame for the distressing cultural success—as shown by the bestseller lists—of this slander falls squarely on the Bush White House. It contributed immensely to the howling of the jackals by issuing a wrong-headed apology on a highly convoluted controversy involving a disputed piece of intelligence.

★

In July 2003, the White House disavowed a single sentence which was spoken in the State of the Union address eight months earlier. The sentence in question was: "The British Government has learned that Saddam Hussein recently sought significant quantities of uranium from Africa."

The disavowal came after a day in which reporters grilled soon-to-be-departed White House press secretary Ari Fleischer about the claims of one Joseph C. Wilson IV, a retired foreign-service officer and Clinton administration foreign-policy aide. Eighteen months earlier, at the request of the Central Intelligence Agency, Wilson had gone to the country of Niger—a major source of uranium and a former diplomatic posting of Wilson's—to see what he could find out on the subject. After eight days, during which he drank a lot of tea with a lot of old cronies, Wilson came back and told CIA officials that he could find no evidence that Saddam or his surrogates had sought uranium there.

Between the Wilson trip and the State of the Union Address eleven months later, the British government said it had uncovered intelligence that Saddam had sought uranium in Africa. Some of the documents used by the British—those involving Niger—later turned out to have been forged. Still, the British insisted they had evidence other than the forgeries to indicate that Saddam was reconstituting his nuclear-weapons program by seeking uranium from countries elsewhere in Africa. The matter made its way into the draft of the 2003 State of the Union, and during the vetting process on the speech, the sentence featuring the uranium-in-Africa claim was argued over and massaged and finally carefully worded in such a way that the evidence was sourced to the British.

Wilson went public with the story of his February 2002 mission on the op-ed page of the *New York Times* on July 6, 2003. "Based on my experience with the administration in the months leading up to the war," Wilson wrote, "I have little choice but to conclude that some of the intelligence related to Iraq's nuclear weapons program was twisted to exaggerate the Iraqi threat."[4]

Wilson's own narrative did not justify such a conclusion. He had gone to Niger for little more than a week. He came back and delivered a verbal report to the CIA. He said he had "reason to believe" his report was made known to "appropriate officials" in the government. That was all he had.

Reporters and others made the mistake of conflating Wilson's account with the already well-known story of the forged documents. If the United States possessed intelligence information of our own in February from Wilson, they argued, and if the United States later acknowledged that documents relating to Niger had been forgeries, and still the president went ahead and talked about Saddam's supposed efforts to secure uranium in Africa, then Bush and Company must consciously have known they were stretching the truth. That was precisely what Wilson wanted them to think. "The question now is how that answer was or was not used by our political leadership," he wrote. "If my information was deemed inaccurate, I understand. . . . If, however, the information was ignored because it did not fit certain preconceptions about Iraq, then a legitimate argument can be made that we went to war under false pretenses."

That is a startling logical stretch. In the first place, the information may well have been ignored because nobody in a decision-making position (other than the CIA director George Tenet, perhaps) ever heard about it, even if Wilson said he had "reason to believe" otherwise. For another thing, Wilson drew a conclusion based on an eight-day trip taken as a private citizen. By contrast, British intelligence, with all its resources and after considerable effort, said it had real evidence that Saddam had sought to procure uranium in Africa—not Niger, which was the only country in Africa visited by Wilson, but in Africa generally.

That the United States might choose to accept the conclusions of British intelligence rather than the conclusions of Joseph Wilson does *not* mean that we went to war under false pretenses. The very fact that Wilson could claim such a thing is evidence either of a vanity run amok or—what is clearly the case—a political and ideological mission to invalidate the war with Iraq after the fact.

The day after Wilson's op-ed appeared in the *New York Times,* the White House made the biggest political blunder of the Bush presidency.* "Knowing all that we know now," a senior administration official said, "the reference to Iraq's attempt to acquire

---

* A week after that, some official made the most serious error of the Bush presidency when, in conversation with columnist Robert Novak, the official said that Wilson's wife Valerie Plame worked for the Central Intelligence Agency. It is a crime to knowingly reveal the identity of a covert intelligence operative. The matter lay dormant for two months, then it exploded into the only ongoing political scandal of the presidency. As I write these words in October 2003, an investigation into the leak of Plame's name is underway. It is far from clear that anyone who revealed her identity could have known she was or had been a covert operative, and if no one knew her specific status, the leak was not a violation of law. But it was a colossal screwup, given the firestorm it has created. And if it is somehow proved that the name was leaked with such knowledge, though it is difficult to imagine how such a thing can be proved, then Bush will indeed have his reelection threatened because of it.

uranium from Africa should not have been included in the State of the Union speech."

It appears that someone very senior in the administration believed that since the president was about to take a historic trip to Africa the next day to highlight his $15 billion AIDS initiative, the White House might be able to quiet the controversy by issuing an apology and letting the Africa trip take the spotlight.

This was a fantastically stupid decision. The Africa trip was, in fact, completely overshadowed by the White House admission. The British government responded privately with howls of betrayal—howls that led the administration to try to take back some part of the apology. For a while the White House blamed the CIA for the appearance of the sixteen words in the State of the Union, and Tenet stepped forward (or was pushed forward) to accept responsibility. Then Deputy National Security Adviser Stephen Hadley said it was his fault that the offending line got into the State of the Union, and he offered to resign. The president would not accept Hadley's resignation, but he was furious.

The administration should never have apologized; it had nothing to apologize for. It had accepted an intelligence conclusion drawn by a close ally, and the source of that intelligence was clearly stated in the speech. The White House provided unnecessary fodder for its enemies and, worse, nearly left Tony Blair to reap the whirlwind. The apology stoked a feeding frenzy in England that, in conjunction with a dishonest BBC story about "sexed-up" intelligence and the bizarre suicide of a British weapons expert, almost cost the British prime minister his reputation and his job.

Nothing in this entire story rises to the definition of a "lie." By definition, you cannot "lie" unknowingly. A lie is a conscious attempt to convince others of something you know to be untrue. You can only come to the conclusion that Bush and his people "lied" if you conclude that they never really believed Saddam posed a genuine threat.

That is an insane conclusion. Still, the White House handled the matter so poorly that, in an effort to *prove* just how much the administration believed in the threat, the administration declassified sections of the National Intelligence Estimate for 2002. The NIE is the annual consensus document produced by the executive branch's intelligence agencies. Its conclusions were strong ones. The NIE's authors expressed "high confidence" that Iraq "could make a nuclear weapon in months to a year once it acquires sufficient weapons-grade fissile material."

Further, the document cited "compelling evidence that Saddam is reconstituting a uranium-enrichment effort for Baghdad's nuclear-weapons program." And the majority of security agencies concluded that Iraq, "if left unchecked," would "have a nuclear weapon during this decade."

The NIE included a dissenting footnote, an "alternative view" written by the State Department's intelligence bureau, stating that "the claims of Iraqi pursuit of natural uranium in Africa are, in [the bureau's] assessment, highly dubious."[5] The media, of course, pounced on the footnote, wanting to know why the president and the administration had not committed themselves to the view expressed by the minority rather than the strong conclusions of the majority. That was the complaint as well of John B. Judis and Spencer Ackerman, whose gigantic June 2003 article in the *New Republic,* titled "The Selling of the Iraq War," is essentially the minority version of the National Intelligence Estimate.

"There was no consensus within the American intelligence community that Saddam represented such a grave and imminent threat," they write. This is simply false. There *was* consensus. The consensus was not unanimous in every particular, but consensus need not be unanimous in every particular. For Judis and Ackerman, the arguments made by those who were skeptical of the threat posed by Saddam were self-evidently true and were, just as self-evidently, maliciously shot down by those intent on "politicizing" the intelligence. "The administration," they claim, "ignored, and even suppressed, disagreement within the intelligence agencies and pressured the CIA to reaffirm its preferred version of the Iraqi threat."[6] Their proof for the heinousness of the Bush administration's actions, as in so many of the cases in which the view of Bush critics did not carry the day, is that the consensus document does not reflect the opinions Judis and Ackerman wish that it had. So they simply assert that the disgruntled sources with whom they spoke represented the *true* consensus: "Had the administration accurately depicted the consensus within the intelligence community . . . it would have had a very difficult time convincing Congress and the American public to support a war to disarm Saddam."

Judis and Ackerman make a great deal out of the fact that Vice President Dick Cheney said on NBC's *Meet the Press* that Saddam Hussein "has, in fact, reconstituted nuclear weapons." They are right that this statement was almost surely untrue and did *not* reflect the consensus of the intelligence community. But as the fine Washington reporter Stephen Hayes points out in the *Weekly Standard,* "it seems likely that Cheney misspoke. He presumably meant to echo President Bush, who had said that there was evidence Iraq was reconstituting its nuclear *program.* At least three other times in the same interview—never cited in the *New Republic*—Cheney was clear the worry about nuclear weapons was in the future."[7]

It may indeed be true that Bush and Blair and their staffs were willing to believe the worst of Saddam Hussein, and that the worst turned out not to be true. But they did so in good faith, backed by the assessments of their intelligence agencies.

It is easy to misunderstand and overestimate the work of intelligence agencies. It is their job to collect bits of information, often with great difficulty. Those bits of information are then collated and painstakingly analyzed to figure out how they fit together as a whole. Intelligence is an amalgam of art, science, and guesswork. As a result, it is often wrong or blind. Consider the fact that we attempted on three occasions during the Iraq war to kill Saddam Hussein with massive bombs based on so-called hard intelligence—the best kind, the kind offered by an eyewitness—only to learn that Saddam had probably not been in those locations.

Often, all too often, leaders are forced to make a judgment based on incomplete information. In the case of Saddam Hussein and his weapons-of-mass-destruction programs, the judgment made by the United States and Britain that he represented a threat was a deduction. Saddam Hussein had essentially kicked U.N. inspectors out of Iraq in 1998. There would be no reason to believe he had chosen to destroy his remaining weaponry without informing the international community of this action—since Hussein could have ended all international sanctions against him in one fell swoop had he done so. When he was president, Bill Clinton believed Saddam Hussein was actively developing weapons of mass destruction. So did the United Nations. They believed it because it would have been wishful thinking to believe otherwise.

In the run-up to the war, the Bush administration was attempting to convey its sense of alarm at the prospects of a nuclear Iraq and at the chance that Iraq might figure out a way to use chemical and biological weapons against the United States. As we have seen before, the most effective delivery vehicle for such weaponry would be an Al-Qaeda suicide bomber, and the administration attempted to convey this possibility as well.

So we come to another area in which those who believe Bush is a liar think they have the goods to prove it. Bush and the administration, they say, have been trying to make the world believe that Saddam Hussein was involved with Al-Qaeda in the September 11 attacks. The critics say the administration knows these allegations are untrue, and yet it continues to peddle them regardless.

In the wake of September 11, some in the administration cited a supposed meeting between Iraqi intelligence and Al-Qaeda hijacker Mohammad Atta. On *Meet the Press* in December 2001, Vice President Cheney said, "It's been pretty well confirmed that [Atta] did go to Prague and he did meet with a senior official of the Iraqi intelligence service in Czechoslovakia last April, several months before the attack."[8]

Since then, doubt has been cast on the veracity of this piece of intelligence, largely because it comes from a single source. Judis and Ackerman describe him as a "single unreliable witness." But in the *Weekly Standard,* Stephen Hayes counters: "Assessments of the reliability of the witness vary, with some high-ranking Czech officials insisting to this day that the meeting took place. It is fair to say the alleged Atta meeting was disputed, but it's hardly accurate to imply that officials were unanimous in their belief that it didn't happen."⁹

In addition, FBI director Robert Mueller has said his agency has been unable to find evidence that Atta traveled outside the United States in the spring of 2001. This fact is used as evidence to prove Atta couldn't have been in Prague, but of course he could have taken the trip using a false passport. A defiant Cheney has continued to mention the Atta-Iraq link, even though he acknowledges that it is "unconfirmed."

No one in the administration has ever said—*ever*—that Iraq was involved in the planning or execution of the 9/11 attacks. As Michael Anton of the National Security Council told the *Boston Globe*, "It's not an alliance. It was midlevel contacts, in some cases high-level contacts, going back a decade. That's a fact. No one's ever debunked it." Those contacts include meetings between Bin Laden and the head of Iraqi intelligence in Sudan in the 1990s and the presence in Northern Iraq of an Al-Qaeda offshoot called Ansar Al-Islam.

Judis and Ackerman say the Bush administration claimed to have "evidence" that Iraq had participated in "joint exercises with Al-Qaeda" when no such exercises ever took place. But no administration official has *ever* claimed there had been "joint exercises"—a term that in any case usually refers to war games played together by the armies of two separate countries.

The administration has said that an Al-Qaeda terrorist named Abu Musab Zarkawi was wounded in the war in Afghanistan fighting against the United States. He went to Baghdad for medical treatment in May 2002—treatment that could not have taken place, administration officials believe, without Saddam Hussein's say-so.

Zarkawi had a terror network in operation in Iraq. Its existence was uncovered in April 2003 when the United States arrested one of Zarkawi's operatives near Baghdad, and there is some evidence that Zarkawi may have masterminded the assassination of U.S. diplomat Laurence Foley in Jordan in October 2002.

Even Vince Cannistraro, a former CIA counterintelligence chief who believes it is "absurd" to think that Saddam was "promoting al-Qaeda" does say "that there was a tolerance for a Zarkawi network in Iraq seems clear."[10] If Saddam was "tolerating" a Zarkawi network, then why is it "absurd" to imagine Saddam was promoting Al-Qaeda? Apparently because a Zarkawi associate in custody at Guantanamo Bay claims his operation was independent of Al-Qaeda's.

Some intelligence officials believe that Zarkawi is indeed independent. And that's more than enough for David Corn of the *Nation* to argue that Bush "lied large and small, directly and by omission. . . . Bush asserted that Iraq was 'harboring a terrorist network, headed by a senior Al Qaeda terrorist planner'; U.S. intelligence officials told reporters this terrorist was operating outside of Al Qaeda control."[11]

Let us assume for a moment that these unnamed "intelligence officials"—who, by the way, use leftist journalists like Judis, Walter Pincus of the *Washington Post,* and Seymour Hersh of the *New Yorker* as their conduits, and ought therefore to be presumed to be grinding axes left, left, and farther left—were correct and Bush was wrong.

Under what understanding of the word "lie" is Bush therefore a liar? Once again, by definition, a liar is someone who utters something he knows to be false. Corn has an answer to this seemingly insuperable problem with calling Bush a liar. Even though the intelligence Bush received was circumstantial, he spoke sentences like this one: "intelligence gathered by this and other governments leaves no doubt that the Iraq regime continues to possess and conceal some of the most lethal weapons ever devised."

The intelligence, says Corn, "was not no-doubt stuff." Therefore Bush lies.

But even that is a matter of interpretation. What Bush heard, read, and saw left *him* in "no doubt." It is possible that he drew an erroneous conclusion. Unless and until stockpiles of Iraqi weapons of mass destruction are found—and remember that Hussein could have hidden enough sarin, VX, anthrax, and other chemical agents to kill millions, in a single trailer truck buried somewhere in the desert—the shadow of that possibility will be ever-present.

But to describe questionable certainty as a lie is to do grievous harm to the English language. According to the logic of many who allege that Bush is a liar, if he told you that he thought it would be sunny tomorrow and it rained instead, he would have been telling you a lie. So, for example, Bush is described as a liar or a deceiver because he said his tax cuts would *promote* economic growth and job growth, and as of the fall of 2003, they had only *contributed* to economic growth.

A Web site called Misleader.org features what it calls "a daily chronicle of Bush administration distortion." Among the supposed distortions it chronicles is this one: "Instead of creating 510,000 jobs in 2003, as President Bush predicted, the Republican-led economy has suffered a net loss of 473,000 jobs." This may well be a sobering political fact to be used against Bush in the upcoming election, but it was not a distortion, nor was it misleading in any way. Making a bum prediction doesn't make you a liar—unless, of course, you follow the reasoning of the Washington journalist Joshua Micah Marshall, who has come up with an entirely new conceit to explain why he believes Bush is fundamentally dishonest. "Bush and his administration," he writes, "specialize in a particular form of deception: The confidently expressed, but currently undisprovable assertion."

What do you suppose this means? It means that because Bush believes that the things he wants to do will have helpful and positive consequences, and he says so, he is engaging in a new kind of lie:

> When the president said on numerous occasions that his tax cuts—which were essentially long-term rate reductions for the wealthy—would spur growth without causing structural deficits, most experts . . . cried foul, pointing out both past experience and accepted economic theory said otherwise. But in point of fact nobody could say for sure that maybe this time the cuts might not work. . . . The White House seemed guilty of what might be called persistent, chronic up-is-downism, the tendency to ridicule the possibility that a given policy might actually have its predictable consequences [and] to deny those consequences once they have already occurred. . . . [12]

In short, Bush is a liar because he believes things that Marshall and the "experts" whom Marshall likes do not believe. "To many in the Bush administration," Marshall writes, "the 'experts' look like so many liberals wedded to a philosophy of big government, the welfare state, over-regulation and a pussyfooting role for the nation abroad."

It's true that many in the administration feel that way about a lot of "experts." It's also true that many experts indeed are liberals wedded to a worldview with which the administration disagrees. The administration does have a bias for listening to its own experts, who draw conclusions based on the evidence that differ from the conclusions of the liberals.

It would be nice if running the world were like mathematics, where if you pose the same question to every single person on earth, every single person on earth should be able to come up with the same answer. But it isn't. Experts advise elected politicians. Elected politicians must then act. And unlike the experts, who are rarely sanctioned for giving bad advice or drawing incorrect conclusions, politicians must submit themselves to the sweetest reward or the cruelest punishment: the glory of success and reelection, or the ignominy of defeat and humiliation.

The Bush administration is run by a politician who has political staffers working for him. All politicians sell their policies by presenting the best possible case for them, and try to discount any unfavorable consequences of those policies by finding a different and plausible explanation for those consequences. Politicians will say they're winning when they're losing, and that things are good when they're bad.

In this respect, Bush is no different from any other politician. He and his administration participate in the game known as "spin," and do it pretty well (except in the case of the State of the Union apology). But, to borrow a bit from the logic of Joshua Micah Marshall, it is the job of the "political expert" to recognize the difference between spin and lies. To act as though the two are the same is unadulterated sophism, and it's unworthy of those who seek to make a serious argument against George W. Bush and challenge his legacy as president.

9

"Our Mission and Our Moment"

The war in Iraq has served several purposes. The United States and its allies have ousted a tyrant. We have ended a threat and a potential threat; we have offered hope for the future. Even the quarrels inside the United States over the immense cost of the reconstruction effort have demonstrated our national determination to see through our goal of bringing unalloyed benefits to the Iraqi people—the benefits not only of running water and electricity, but of freedom. "A new regime in Iraq would serve as a dramatic and inspiring example of freedom for other nations in the region," Bush said in February 2003, before going to war. The creation of that new regime is painful and expensive work, but it is a noble as well as a crucial challenge—a grand cause for a great nation using its power to apply the founding principles and precepts of the United States to places in the world where those principles and precepts might appear to have little hope of taking hold.

"It is presumptuous and insulting to suggest that a whole region of the world—or the one-fifth of humanity that is Muslim—is somehow untouched by the most basic aspirations of
life," Bush said in that February 2003 speech. "Human cultures
can be vastly different. Yet the human heart desires the same good
things, everywhere on Earth. In our desire to be safe from brutal
and bullying oppression, human beings are the same. In our desire
to care for our children and give them a better life, we are the
same. For these fundamental reasons, freedom and democracy will
always and everywhere have greater appeal than the slogans of
hatred and the tactics of terror."

Here was something radically new. To demonstrate that the
intervention of the United States in Muslim countries posed no
threat of domination and subjugation, but rather the promise of
political and personal liberation, it became the stated policy of
the United States that the suffering peoples of the Muslim world
deserved to taste the fruits of freedom. No one has ever pushed
the ideals of democratic freedom this far, into terrain this rough.
Though other administrations had made gestures in this direction—Jimmy Carter's stressed the importance of human rights,
Ronald Reagan's stressed the importance of elections—no leader
before Bush had ever conceived of democratization as a worldwide
goal.

How could we manage it? Tyrants fear freedom, and to some
extent we must be able to deal with governments and their leaders
whose systems and methods appall us—if only to protect our
national interests. If we went around talking about democratizing
the world along the principles of the American Constitution, we
might make enemies of the dictators and thugs we sometimes
have to play footsie with.

In addition, there has always been a certain unspoken bias in American foreign-policy circles toward strongmen. The thing about strongmen is, they can be easy to deal with. If a strongman says he'll do something for you, he'll do it; he doesn't have to poll public opinion or push a bill through Congress. Democracy is messy, and spies and cynical State Department diplomats don't like a mess. They like to throw some dollars around, buy some talent, rent a government for a while. And nowhere have they made greater use of this technique than in Muslim countries. Bush is little different in this respect from other presidents. He's had to strike deals with unpleasant fellows, like Pakistan's General Pervez Musharraf, to further the war on terror.

But Bush decided that the need to practice occasional realpolitik would not restrain him from the forthright assertion that American-style democracy is the best form of government and that it would be a blessing for the suffering peoples of the world to live as we live. He refuses to believe that the world cannot be changed for the better, that the better argument, the better government, the better way of life, cannot prevail. The history of the twentieth century is proof that there can be positive change. Realists of a different day had expressed great pessimism about the democratic possibilities for nations that later flowered under freedom, as Bush has observed: "There was a time when many said that the cultures of Japan and Germany were incapable of sustaining democratic values. Well, they were wrong. Some say the same of Iraq today. They are mistaken."

After the fall of the Taliban, Bush did not simply dwell on the defeat of Al-Qaeda. He talked movingly about the emergence of Afghanistan's women from a state of medieval servility at the hands of the Taliban. As he said in early January 2002, "We have liberated a nation from oppression. And we've saved many people from starvation. . . . There is nothing more joyous to my heart than to see our military liberate women who have lived under the most oppressive regime in the history of mankind." The extemporaneous rhetoric here may have been excessive (were the Taliban really more oppressive than the Nazis?), but the very real liberation of Afghanistan's women was central to Bush's vision of the many virtues of the American military intervention. "This cause is noble, and this cause is just," he said. "And we will stay on this cause until we have achieved our objective. [We]'re delivering justice; not revenge, but justice, to agents of terror."

The just cause is not merely the protection of the United States, but also the liberation of suffering peoples. In fighting terrorists, we are not acting out of "revenge." We are in pursuit of justice. What was done to *us* was unjust. What we did to oust those who committed mass murder against us was achieve justice. And trying to better the lives of those we have freed from the yoke of inhuman tyranny is indeed noble. Afghans deserve to live in freedom, in Bush's view, as do the people of Iraq, and as do the Palestinians. They deserve it no less than we do. They deserve to live in freedom because they are, in their very essence as human beings, free.

Here, we can see that Bush's vision of the post–September 11 world has been given uncommon heft and power by the depth and strength of his religious convictions and his understanding of the transcendent idea that gave birth and life to this country. The freedom in which Bush believes is the free will granted to all people by God—as best and most powerfully expressed by the founding American creed that "we are endowed by our Creator with certain unalienable rights, that among these are life, liberty and the pursuit of happiness."

That gift of freedom is universal. Freedom is the natural state of the human condition. The "we" who were "endowed by our Creator" aren't only Americans (indeed, we had to fight a civil war to make that clear even inside the boundaries of our own country). The "we" of the Declaration of Independence refers to all humankind—Muslims and Jews, atheists and Buddhists, Zoroastrians and Latter-day Saints.

If, at the end of our struggles, we bring democracy to Iraq and Palestine and the rest of the Muslim world, we will only be helping to establish *institutions* of freedom. In Bush's eyes, God already did the most important work before the beginning of time. "Americans are a free people, who know that freedom is the right of every person and the future of every nation," Bush said at the conclusion of his 2002 State of the Union address. "The liberty we prize is not America's gift to the world, it is God's gift to humanity."

★

The splendor of Bush's rhetoric in that moment has been equaled time and again in the course of his presidency. Every element of his vision—a vision of an America overturning the new reality and replacing it with one that might assure our safety and improve the lives in those swamps where the contagion has been festering—was there in the hours and days following the 9/11 attacks. And it has been explicated in a series of presidential addresses that have lifted Bush to the very first rank of presidents when it comes to communicating with the American people.

It is already a cliché to say that George W. Bush "rose to the occasion" in the ten days following September 11, that an ineloquent man was suddenly gifted with a golden tongue and a pitch-perfect sense of what the American people needed to hear and what the world needed to see from the United States. When he stood atop the rubble of the World Trade Center with a megaphone and spontaneously told a shouting crowd, "I can hear you, the world hears you, and the people who knocked these buildings down will hear all of us soon," he instantly ascended from the prosaic to the prophetic.

It's worth recalling just how incredibly complex a rhetorical task he was faced with in those days. In the immediate aftermath, Bush had to speak to the nation, for the nation, and about the nation to the world. He had to be a eulogist and a source of comfort. That much was obvious. But if he dwelled on his role as the spokesman for national grief, he would have run the risk of deepening the sorrow. Worse yet, he would have risked appearing weak at precisely the moment that American weakness could have convinced terrorists they had succeeded in breaking the country's will, giving them the impetus to strike again and again with impunity.

An incredibly delicate balance was needed—a balance between loss and grief, between gratitude for national unity and the determination to face down those who had committed mass murder on American soil, between paying tribute to the enduring value of the freedom for which we had been attacked and to the democratic principles that are so noxious to those who would defeat us. And it all had to be expressed just so.

There's a fine line between righteous anger and self-righteous rage, between a call for justice and a thirst for vengeance. Anger against foreign enemies responsible for the evil was justified; anger against American Muslims who had nothing to do with it was not. "I ask you," our president said, "to uphold the values of

America, and remember why so many have come here. We are in a fight for our principles, and our first responsibility is to live by them. No one should be singled out for unfair treatment or unkind words because of their ethnic background or religious faith."

He struck this near-miraculous balance word by word, sentence by sentence, appearance by appearance. We were as one in our heartbreak: "Grief and tragedy and hatred are only for a time. Goodness, remembrance, and love have no end, and the Lord of life holds all who die and all who mourn. It is said that adversity introduces us to ourselves. This is true of a nation as well. In this trial, we have been reminded, and the world has seen, that our fellow Americans are generous and kind, resourceful and brave." And we were united in our grief, our outrage, and our sense that we had been attacked because we were good—and that our enemies had attacked us because they were evil.

In his speech before a joint session of Congress on September 20, 2001—the greatest presidential address of my lifetime—Bush convinced a weakened nation that it was in fact strong: "We have seen the state of our Union in the endurance of rescuers, working past exhaustion. We have seen the unfurling of flags, the lighting of candles, the giving of blood, the saying of prayers—in English, Hebrew, and Arabic. We have seen the decency of a loving and giving people who have made the grief of strangers their own."

In that strength, he saw righteous purpose. "Tonight we are a country awakened to danger and called to defend freedom," he said. "Our grief has turned to anger, and anger to resolution. Whether we bring our enemies to justice, or bring justice to our enemies, justice will be done."

And in that righteous resolution, he found the reason and purpose of his presidency: "I will not forget this wound to our country or those who inflicted it. I will not yield; I will not rest; I will not relent in waging this struggle for freedom and security for the American people. The course of this conflict is not known, yet its outcome is certain."

The power of Bush's formal presidential addresses represents the final demonstration of his standing as a true visionary. He has delivered at least six[1] that will be studied by those who want to understand how a president can successfully talk to the American people and the world. He has used the bully pulpit to guide the American people through the new reality, in which new presidential policies and a new presidential attitude are required to preserve, protect, and defend the Constitution of the United States. How has he done it? He hired well, for one thing, working closely for years now with a team of splendid writers, led by Michael Gerson. But that's not a sufficient explanation. After all, both his father and Jimmy Carter had some very fine writers working for them, and their presidential speeches were nothing short of awful. Bush's own solecisms—the way he adds unnecessary syllables to words and stumbles over the simplest and shortest of them—seemed likely to cause him some rhetorical grief as president.

Bush realized after September 11 that the deadly seriousness the job required also required him to master the techniques of a great presidential speaker. The nation needed a leader; the world needed to respect and fear the American president. At such a time, that leadership, that respect and that fear, could only be conveyed through words. So he set himself to the task with his extraordinary self-discipline—reading and rereading his speeches endlessly, practicing them, slowing himself down, concentrating.

The speaker who has emerged from these exercises is a solemn man who wishes to make sure his listeners understand and comprehend every word. And yet he does not talk down to them. The language he uses in his major addresses is elevated, formal, and elegantly rendered. He delivers them conversationally. There is a lot of God-talk, but he does not sound preachy. In his extemporaneous speeches, by contrast, Bush is jokey, slangy, terrifically informal. But the key impressions he conveys in his formal addresses are earnestness and gravity—the perfect tone for an uncertain and frightening age.

★

Time and again, Bush has captured the American soul and spirit in transforming ways. A few lesser-noted examples: Following the tragic destruction of the space shuttle *Columbia* on February 1, 2003, Bush spoke to the American people. He had a difficult task; first, because of the gruesome nature of the event and, second, because he would be going up against the memory of Ronald Reagan's now-canonical four-minute speech that followed the explosion of the *Challenger* space shuttle in 1986.

He was up to the task. "This cause of exploration and discovery is not an option we choose; it is a desire written in the human heart," he said. "Mankind is led into the darkness beyond our world by the inspiration of discovery and the longing to understand. Our journey into space will go on.

"In the skies today we saw destruction and tragedy. Yet farther than we can see there is comfort and hope. In the words of the prophet Isaiah, 'Lift your eyes and look to the heavens. Who created all these? He who brings out the starry hosts one by one and calls them each by name. Because of His great power and mighty strength, not one of them is missing.'

"The same Creator who names the stars also knows the names

of the seven souls we mourn today. The crew of the shuttle *Columbia* did not return safely to Earth; yet we can pray that all are safely home."

Three months after September 11, at exactly the moment of the attack on the first tower, Bush spoke to the nation: "For those of us who lived through these events, the only marker we'll ever need is the tick of a clock at the forty-sixth minute of the eighth hour of the eleventh day. We will remember where we were and how we felt. We will remember the dead and what we owe them. We will remember what we lost and what we found. And in our time, we will honor the memory of the eleventh day by doing our duty as citizens of this great country, freedom's home and freedom's defender."

On the one-year anniversary of September 11, he spoke again in terms of freedom and the human spirit. "There is a line in our time, and in every time, between those who believe all men are created equal, and those who believe that some men and women and children are expendable in the pursuit of power," he said. "There is a line in our time, and in every time, between the defenders of human liberty and those who seek to master the minds and souls of others. Our generation has now heard history's call, and we will answer it. . . .

"A milestone is passed, and a mission goes on. Be confident. Our country is strong. And our cause is even larger than our country. Ours is the cause of human dignity; freedom guided by conscience and guarded by peace. This ideal of America is the hope of all mankind. That hope drew millions to this harbor. That hope still lights our way. And the light shines in the darkness. And the darkness will not overcome it."

On June 1, 2001, in the West Point commencement address

in which he unveiled the doctrine of preemption, Bush revealed how his worldview runs far deeper and is far more sophisticated than the more self-consciously sophisticated efforts to explain away the actions of terrorists and murderers:

"Some worry that it is somehow undiplomatic or impolite to speak the language of right and wrong. I disagree. Different circumstances require different methods, but not different moralities. Moral truth is the same in every culture, in every time, and in every place. Targeting innocent civilians for murder is always and everywhere wrong. Brutality against women is always and everywhere wrong. There can be no neutrality between justice and cruelty, between the innocent and the guilty. We are in a conflict between good and evil, and America will call evil by its name. By confronting evil and lawless regimes, we do not create a problem, we reveal a problem. And we will lead the world in opposing it."

★

This visionary president's efforts in the here and now—in the time since September 11—have already changed the world for the better. The world's leading terrorist organization has been mortally wounded, and its network of support and its developing assets inside the United States have been disrupted. Two of the world's worst regimes have been removed, and Saddam Hussein has been captured. And after the displays of American military power and strategy in the Afghan and Iraq wars, after it had become clear that the United States could indeed win wars without causing massive civilian casualties while losing very few of its own troops, the nation's authority was enhanced in ways we don't even yet quite understand. We got a sense of it during the crisis in the African nation of Liberia in the summer of 2003—where after months of U.N. and international pressure, the merest whiff of possible American involvement caused its dictator, Charles Taylor, to give up power.

There is an idea abroad in the land that an America with enhanced authority and unquestioned power might make itself a greater and more tempting target for its enemies. The evidence for this is that American soldiers in Iraq have been targeted for hit-and-run attacks by remnants of Saddam Hussein's regime and others who want to engage with Americans. Every death of an American soldier is a wound to the nation. But these attacks are meaningless strategically. They do not affect the overall image of the United States as the world's foremost power—willing to engage in battle when attacked and willing, if necessary, to engage in efforts to change the circumstances and the ideologies that gave rise to those attacks.

Nevertheless, the strikes against American forces in Iraq are not meaningless psychologically. As with all terrorist attacks, their intent is to demoralize. The terrorists want to instill fear in the United States so that the fear will instill doubt—doubt that there will be a final and total victory, doubt that the mission was valid in the first place.

Whether the attacks have that effect is entirely up to us. We can choose to understand that casualty figures in Iraq are startlingly low for any major military conflict in the course of human history—and that a death toll of a few soldiers a week in a military force of 150,000 is not a catastrophe. Or we can choose to believe that the United States has gotten bogged down in a quagmire, that the war in Iraq was unnecessary and that the cost of rebuilding Iraq is too high.

The Iraq war's validity is also at issue because a cache of weapons of mass destruction did not turn up in the wake of the war. Democratic Senators Edward Kennedy and Robert Byrd have led their party's charge in claiming that the missing weapons prove the threat from Iraq was not "imminent" and therefore the war was retroactively unjustified.

But it is important to note, and never to forget, that the president did not say Iraq posed an "imminent" threat. The entire concept behind the Iraq war was to eliminate the threat posed by Saddam Hussein *before* it became imminent. At the end of the Gulf War, the United States and the United Nations imposed a regime of sanctions on Iraq designed to make it as difficult as possible for Saddam Hussein to function normally. That sanctions regime was breaking down by 2001. To help stave off a humanitarian crisis, the United Nations had allowed Iraq to participate in a so-called oil-for-food program, the end result of which was that the Baathist regime had been able to regain oil revenues even as it continued to starve its own people. Those oil revenues represented the first real breach of the sanctions regime, and France and Russia, among others, were continually pressing the United Nations to open Iraq up still more.

There is every reason to believe that, absent U.S. action, the sanctions regime would not have held in place through this decade. The dam would have burst, oil revenue would have begun pouring in—and at that point the threat that was not imminent would have become imminent in an instant.

Those who choose to believe that Saddam Hussein posed no threat in 2002 and would have posed no threat in the future have a right to believe so. But in October 2003, weapons inspector David Kay declared flatly that "we have discovered dozens of

WMD-related program activities and significant amounts of equipment that Iraq concealed from the United Nations during the inspections that began in late 2002," including "a clandestine network of laboratories and safehouses within the Iraqi Intelligence Service that contained equipment subject to UN monitoring and suitable for continuing [weapons of mass destruction] research."[2]

They found evidence of continuing research into ricin and aflatoxin, two of the earth's most poisonous substances, and "new research on [biological warfare] agents, Brucella and Congo Crimean Hemorrhagic Fever."

Scientists had in their homes "documents and equipment . . . that would have been useful in resuming uranium enrichment" necessary for the eventual construction of nuclear weapons. Nuclear weapons need to be delivered on rockets, and Kay's team also found "plans and advanced design work for new long-range missiles with ranges up to at least 1000 km—well beyond the 150 km range limit imposed by the UN. Missiles of a 1000 km range would have allowed Iraq to threaten targets throughout the Middle East, including Ankara, Cairo, and Abu Dhabi."

And, in a chilling piece of evidence that the phrase "axis of evil" wasn't just a speechwriter's fancy, Kay said he had uncovered "clandestine attempts between late 1999 and 2002 to obtain from North Korea technology related to 1,300 km range ballistic missiles . . . , 300 km range anti-ship cruise missiles, and other prohibited military equipment."

It is a tragic fact, but a fact nonetheless, that most of the leading lights of the Democratic Party and many of the nation's liberal intellectuals have committed themselves to a campaign to convince the American people that the Iraq war was not noble, not useful, not an advance in human history, but a mistake and a failure. It was neither. It was a brilliant tactical and strategic stroke, a proper use of American military power in the service of good, and a wondrous success.

To the extent that the attack on Bush is purely partisan, all one can say is: that's life. Democrats want a Democrat in the White House, and that can only happen if the American people turn on George W. Bush. Democrats see it as their job to make that happen, and while many of their attacks are unfair,[3] they are justified by the warp-and-woof of American politics.

The *ideological* attack against Bush, however, is a different matter. Those who have argued out of deep conviction that Bush is a fool, a puppet, a fanatic, a Hitler-like figure, a betrayer of civil liberties out to end all social programs, a crazy cowboy, and a bald-faced liar have been infected with a strain of dementia that has been a part of American political life since the nation's founding. They are guilty of the depersonalizing of someone with whom they disagree—of assuming that those who believe something different from what they believe are somehow lacking in any virtue and therefore less than human. This disease (to which ideological conservatives, alas, are as susceptible as ideological liberals) distorts perception, destroys reason, and makes rational discussion very nearly impossible.

But because I believe America is the nation George W. Bush evoked in those indescribable days after September 11, I believe that Americans are inoculated against the most vicious strains of this disease. I believe they still agree with the president who said on September 20, 2001, that "in our grief and anger we have found our mission and our moment. Freedom and fear are at war. The advance of human freedom—the great achievement of our time, and the great hope of every time—now depends on us. Our nation—this generation—will lift a dark threat of violence from our people and our future. We will rally the world to this cause by our efforts, by our courage. We will not tire, we will not falter, and we will not fail."

George W. Bush has laid out the path this country must take if it is to be secure, and the first steps we've taken down this long road are worthy of celebration. The celebration should be sober, even somber, as befits the challenges of the present moment, the difficulties that lie ahead, and the grieving that still goes on for those lost in the war on terror. But America has done some extraordinary and wonderful things these past three years.

Bush Country has found its calling.

Acknowledgments

Acknowledgments have lately become a printed version of the Oscar speech we sorry book authors know we will never get to deliver. So let me keep this short before the orchestra in your head begins to play me off the page.

I owe an enormous debt to my colleagues at the *New York Post*—particularly Bob McManus, a newspaperman's newspaperman and one of nature's noblemen. Rupert Murdoch's passionate commitment to the expression of views that are unconventional in the mainstream media have earned him the enmity of many of the same people who criticize George W. Bush. I have been involved with three of Rupert's contributions to the national debate for a decade now—the revived *Post,* the *Weekly Standard,* and the Fox News Channel. My debt to him is inexpressible.

The Hoover Institution on War, Revolution and Peace gave me shelter and succor as a media fellow while I hurried to finish this book. The time I have spent in and around the Hoover Tower on the Stanford University campus over the past decade has been among the most productive of my career. I am grateful to Hoover's director, John Raisian; to Hoover stalwarts David Brady, Peter Robinson, Tom Henriksen, Mandy MacCalla, and the wondrous Arnold Beichman; and to my oldest friend, Tod Lindberg, for being Tod Lindberg.

Every page of this book has been improved by the editorial recommendations of Midge Decter, otherwise known as Midge Podhoretz, otherwise known as my mother. I can't really turn to my father, Norman Podhoretz, for such nuts-and-bolts editorial criticism—because even though he is one of the great editors and critics of our time, when it comes to his children, critical words rarely appear in his vocabulary. Which is a wonderful gift of a different sort.

Andrew Ferguson was remarkably generous with his time and writerly advice. Daniel Casse and Stephen Hayes made valuable suggestions. Cheryl Miller's diligent research was of immeasurable help. Roberta Roth offered quiet enlightenment.

My agents, Glen Hartley and Lynn Chu, were indefatigable, and found me a happy home at St. Martin's Press. Tim Bent, my meticulous and wonderfully literate editor, has been a joy to work with.

My wife, Ayala, thought up the title. She thereby made this book better. But then, she has made every aspect of my life better and fuller and richer, as she has filled it with wisdom and grace and love.

Notes

1. Energy in the Executive

1. Mary McGrory, "Leaving Conservationists Cold," *Washington Post,* August 2, 2001.

2. Transcript, Democratic Presidential Debate, September 9, 2003.

3. Paul Krugman, "Duped and Betrayed," *New York Times,* June 6, 2003.

4. Jules Lobel and Michael Ratner, "The End," in *Power Trip: U.S. Unilateralism and Global Strategy After September 11,* edited by John Feffer (Seven Stories Press, 2003), p. 55.

5. Michael Lind, *Made in Texas* (Basic Books, 2003), p. 160.

6. Robert Scheer, "A Firm Basis for Impeachment," *Los Angeles Times,* July 15, 2003.

7. Harold Meyerson, "The Most Dangerous President Ever," *American Prospect,* June 2003.

8. Norman Mailer, "The White Man Unburdened," *New York Review of Books,* July 17, 2003.

9. She didn't even have the minimal courage to admit she'd said it, but Chancellor Gerhard Schroeder implicitly acknowledged the truth when he got her to resign.

Crazy Liberal Idea #1: Bush Is a Moron

1. Transcript, *Equal Time,* MSNBC, June 14, 2000.
2. The "z" in "president" is Begala's little joke. Very little.
3. Quoted in Frank Bruni, *Ambling Into History* (HarperCollins, 2002), p. 40.
4. I must admit that I was guilty of this trope as well. I supported John McCain in the Republican primary and wrote a column for the *New York Post* in which I ridiculed Bush's verbal solecisms: "So to my fellow conservatives, I say: At least John McCain knows how to speak English!" Boy, is my face red.
5. Todd Gitlin, "It's the Stupidity, Stupid," *Salon.com,* October 24, 2000.
6. "GW Bush: The Man Is Stupid," *Independent,* June 16, 2002.
7. Manuel Roig-Franzia, "Changed by Terror, a Nice Guy Converted," *Washington Post,* July 27, 2003.
8. Note the unnecessary and ungrammatical comma after the word "but" and the ungrammatical singular-plural problem. People who accuse others of stupidity should probably not reveal their own so easily.
9. "The Mediocrity That Roared," *Salon.com,* November 23, 1999.
10. Byron York, "Annals of Bush-Hating," *National Review,* September 4, 2003.
11. Garry Trudeau, intro., *More George W. Bushisms,* edited by Jacob Weisberg (Fireside Books, 2002), p. vii.
12. Andrew Ferguson, "Reporter's Portrayal of Bush Puts Forth Puzzling Paradox," *Los Angeles Business Journal,* February 25, 2002.
13. Bruni, p. 126.
14. Jacob Weisberg, ed., *George W. Bushisms* (Fireside Books, 2001), p. 93.
15. Bruni, p. 123.
16. Trudeau, pp. vii–viii.
17. Jonathan Chait, "Presumed Ignorant," *New Republic,* April 30, 2001.
18. Maureen Dowd, "Cheney Stays in the Picture," *New York Times,* August 11, 2002.
19. Don Hazen, "Bush Speak: An Interview with Mark Crispin Miller," *Alternet.org,* June 5, 2001.
20. The phrase "amiable dunce" was Democratic éminence grise Clark Clifford's dismissive description of Ronald Reagan.
21. Dana Milbank, "In Game of Expectations, Bush Usually Wins," *Washington Post,* June 8, 2003.

2. Voyage 'Round His Father

1. Nelson Rockefeller was appointed vice president by Gerald Ford, himself an appointed vice president, which makes Nelson the least official American official of the twentieth century.

2. Bush did his full National Guard service, with gaps of time when he was out of state working on political campaigns. He made up the time later. He was given an expedited release from the guard when he moved to Boston to attend Harvard Business School. It may be that he received some preferential treatment because of his last name, although a Yale University graduate applying for a space in the Texas Air National Guard in 1968 would have seemed like a pretty good candidate no matter what his last name was. But the entire pseudo-scandal surrounding his service is hypocritical in the extreme. Those who claim to be upset about it didn't mind the fact that Bill Clinton skipped his service entirely, nor do they think that those who avoided the draft did anything wrong (though they love to beat their breasts about it from the safe perch of decades later). They're just looking for anything that adds to their indictment of Bush, no matter whether it agrees with or contradicts their own principles.

3. Lois Romano and George Lardner Jr., "Following his Father's Path, Step by Step by Step," *Washington Post,* July 27, 1999.

4. Bill Minutaglio, *First Son: George W. Bush and the Family Dynasty* (Three Rivers Press, 2001), p. 85.

5. Joe Drape, "In the Fish Bowl with Little George," *Chicago Tribune,* May 1, 1992.

6. Quoted in Minutaglio, p. 210.

7. Chris Matthews, "W Shocks Detractors, Rises to Challenge," *The Hill,* December 5, 2001.

8. Jeff Greenfield, quoted in transcript, *CNN Special Report with Aaron Brown,* CNN, October 11, 2001.

9. David Gergen, delivering the Landon Lecture at the Kansas State University, November 2, 2001.

10. "Sore Winners," *New Republic,* December 5, 1988; quoted in Minutaglio, p. 232.

11. "Bush's Eldest Son Relishes Role as a Texas Delegate," *Houston Chronicle,* August 16, 1988; quoted in Minutaglio, p. 230.

12. Ibid.

13. "Brothers Bush: All in the Political Family," *Austin American Statesman*, October 25, 1998; quoted in Minutaglio, p. 317.

14. Skip Hollandsworth, "Born to Run," *Texas Monthly*, May 1994.

15. *Texas Monthly*, May 1994.

16. Quoted in Frank Bruni, *Ambling Into History* (HarperCollins, 2002), p. 148.

17. Interview with Tom Brokaw, NBC News, April 25, 2003.

18. Francis Bacon, "Of Great Place," *Essays or Counsels*. The essay can be found on the World Wide Web at http://fly.hiwaay.net/~paul/bacon/essays/place.html.

19. Or, rather, Karen Hughes says it. *A Charge to Keep* is an unusual campaign book in that it makes no bones about the fact that Bush didn't write it even though his name is on the cover. His chief communications adviser, Karen Hughes, is the book's author, and even got to write a little author's note of her own. It's not a good book, to put it mildly. In a hilarious evisceration of the book, Andrew Ferguson dubbed its author "Bush/Hughes" and wrote: "As Bush/Hughes note in the introduction, *A Charge to Keep* was written primarily to preempt the work of other biographers. George W. Bush has told his story here, and he's told it first. From now on, any contradictory accounts that other writers may offer up will therefore have to be squared with Bush's original rendering. This will, in turn, be impossible, partly because his own story-telling is so vague and discontinuous, and partly because no reader, having read *A Charge to Keep*, will remember anything about it." But it did break perverse new ground in the honesty with which Bush acknowledges he wasn't its author.

20. George W. Bush, *A Charge to Keep* (William Morrow, 1999), p. 184.

21. Ibid., p. 185.

22. In relative terms, John F. Kennedy's tax cut in 1962 was the largest, followed by Ronald Reagan's in 1981. But because the economy is twice the size it was in 1981, Bush's tax cut has a larger dollar amount attached to it.

Crazy Liberal Idea #2: Bush Is a Puppet

1. Maureen Dowd, "Deja Dubya," *New York Times*, February 18, 2001.

2. I must confess once again that I was guilty of using the same argument in a *New York Post* column published January 18, 2000, titled "Meet George W.'s Brain." Soon after I wrote a column titled "Why McCain Will Smash Bush." I've had better months.

3. James Moore and Wayne Slater, *Bush's Brain* (John Wiley and Sons, 2003), p. 12.

4. The only insider account that has ever seemed to hint at Rove's dominance came from John DiIulio, the brilliant academic who was asked by Bush to run his faith-based initiative in 2001. DiIulio left after six months and later sent an e-mail to an *Esquire* reporter referring to Rove as a "Mayberry Machiavelli" who made every decision at the White House and did so based on political calculations. As it happens, I know John DiIulio very well. I was his editor for several years, and I consider him a friend. Everyone who knows him knows that he's a bit of a hothead—a man supremely assured of the vital, world-historic importance of whatever task he has undertaken to perform. The faith-based initiative ran into political trouble earlier because of profound practical problems—the Left was screaming about the intrusion of religion into the public sector, while the Right and religious groups were finding it nearly impossible to reconcile their core convictions with some of the compromises they would have to make to receive government moneys. The experience was understandably frustrating for DiIulio, but it's simply a matter of fact that White Houses have to make choices on where they will spend political capital and which fights it is worth having at which times. His "Mayberry Machiavelli" e-mail was intemperate in exactly the way DiIulio is often lovably intemperate— and must be understood not as a description of fact but rather as a bleat of disappointment and frustration. DiIulio acknowledged as much when he apologized for having sent the e-mail to *Esquire*.

5. "The Eyes of the Nation Are Upon You," *St. Petersburg Times,* May 19, 1997; quoted in Minutaglio, *First Son,* p. 308.

6. Simon Schama, "The Dead and the Guilty," *Guardian,* September 11, 2002.

7. Paul Krugman, "The Great Divide," *New York Times,* January 29, 2002.

8. For the record, Elliott Abrams is my brother-in-law.

9. Michael Lind, "How the Neoconservatives Conquered Washington— And Launched a War," *New Statesman,* April 10, 2003. And actually, no, Bush never said and never believed that the threat from Saddam was "imminent," as we shall see in chapters 8 and 9.

3. Return to Reaganism

1. By "some conservatives," I mean "me." I made this argument in a spec-
tacularly stupid article I published in the *Times* (London) for which I was properly made fun of by Andrew Sullivan and others.

2. Paul Light, "The Winner's Short Transition Spells Trouble," *Boston
Globe,* December 12, 2000.

3. Bush would recast this policy again two years later, when he decided to
take on global AIDS. See chapter 6.

4. "George W. Bush's Project," in Steven E. Schier, ed., *High Risk and Big
Ambition* (University of Pittsburgh Press, 2004).

Crazy Liberal Idea #3: Bush Is a Fanatic

1. Henri Tincq, "The Clash of Two Fundamentalisms," *Le Monde,* March
31, 2003.

2. Quoted in "Bush's Messiah Complex," *Progressive,* February 2003.

3. C. Welton Gaddy, "The President's Irresponsible Use of Religious Language," Religion and Culture Communications Initiative Audio News Conference, February 11, 2003.

4. Karen Armstrong, "Our Role in Terror," *Guardian,* September 18,
2003.

5. John Esposito interview with *Asiasource.org,* May 13, 2002.

6. Elaine Pagels, "On the President's Irresponsible Use of Religious Language," Religion and Culture Communications Initiative Audio News Conference, February 11, 2003.

7. "Reckoning with Armageddon," *New York Times,* October 25, 1984.

8. Rod Dreher, "Evangelicals and Jews Together," *National Review,* June
5, 2002.

9. Quoted in "Bush's Messiah Complex," *Progressive.*

10. Quoted in "Bush's Messiah Complex," *Progressive.*

11. Joe Klein, "The Blinding Glare of His Certainty," *Time,* February 18,
2003.

12. Many of my fellow Jews remain fearful of Bush, despite the fact that
he may be the most philo-Semitic and certainly the most pro-Israel president
ever elected. Some of that fear is due to a story Bush's mother tells about a
discussion they had in which he said Jews would not go to heaven because they

had not accepted Christ into their hearts. Barbara Bush called Billy Graham, who told her that God will decide who gets into heaven, not mortal man—and that answer was good enough for Bush, who hasn't questioned it since. Jews keep raising this question, and they are foolish to do so. After all, Jews don't believe in the Christian heaven, so what would it matter whether or not someone like Bush thinks or doesn't think we'll be there? What matters is how a non-Jew acts towards Jews. And Bush is a great friend to Jews.

4. Before September 11

1. Quoted in Carl M. Cannon, "Judging Bush," *National Journal,* June 6, 2003.
2. Carl M. Cannon, "Uncivil Liberties," *National Journal,* September 20, 2003.
3. Quoted in Kate O'Beirne, "Weak Non-Reformer," *National Review,* May 28, 2001.
4. Chester E. Finn Jr., "Leaving Education Reform Behind," *Weekly Standard,* January 14, 2002.
5. He did neutralize Forbes, but it turned out Forbes wasn't the threat in New Hampshire; John McCain was.
6. Formal notification of the U.S. withdrawal did not come until December 2001 and was not legally effective until May 2002.
7. Statistics quoted by the National Center for Policy Analysis, 1997.
8. Quoted in Cannon, "Judging Bush."

Crazy Liberal Idea #4: Bush Is Hitler . . . Only Not as Talented

1. Robert Kuttner, "Democrats Make Nice While Bush Runs Hard Right," *Boston Globe,* January 7, 2001.
2. Dave Lindorff, "Bush and Hitler: The Strategy of Fear," *Counterpunch.org,* February 2003.
3. Wayne Madsen, "Bush and Hitler: Compare and Contrast," *Counterpunch.org,* January 31, 2003.
4. Edward Jayne, "27 Similarities Between Bush and Hitler," *Dissidentvoice.org,* March 29, 2003.
5. Carlos Fuentes, "Power, Names and Words," *Autodafe.org,* spring 2003.
6. Quoted in John Pilger, "The Big Lie," London *Daily Mirror,* September 22, 2003.

7. Andrew Greeley, "Big Lie on Iraq Comes Full Circle," *Chicago Sun-Times,* September 19, 2003.

8. George Monbiot, "America Is Religion," *Guardian,* July 29, 2003.

9. Kaye Ross, "Nader Calls Bush 'Dictator,' " *San Jose Mercury News,* March 23, 2003. You could certainly say Nader has a lot of nerve complaining, since if he hadn't run for president, Al Gore would surely be in the Oval Office today.

10. All quoted in Will Saletan, "Pious Bias," *Slate.com,* September 15, 2003.

11. Quoted in Beth Gillin, "Increasingly, There's a Furor Over Comparing Bush to the Fuhrer," *Philadelphia Inquirer,* June 18, 2003.

5. Master of the Political Game

1. Bush used this phraseology when he was asked in the summer of 2003 about gay marriage. He was widely misunderstood and attacked for calling homosexuals "sinners," when in fact he was attempting to make the point that, as we are all sinners, people should be careful about condemning the lifestyles of others.

2. Harley Sorensen, "Is Bush a Dry Drunk?" *San Francisco Chronicle,* March 17, 2003.

3. Paul Krugman, who would find it hard to say even that George W. Bush wore a nice-looking tie, wrote one of the most grudging sentences ever crafted on the subject of government largesse in August 2003: "Immediately after 9/11 there was a great national outpouring of sympathy for New York, and a natural inclination to provide generous help. President Bush quickly promised $20 billion, and everyone expected the federal government to assume the burden of additional security. . . . In the end, New York seems to have gotten its $20 billion—barely."

4. That's two-thirds of all households in the United States, according to the Homeownership Alliance.

5. Joint Committee on Taxation, March 6, 2001.

6. Dividends are corporate profits, which are taxed. By taxing the recipient of the dividend as well, the federal government is in effect taking two tax bites out of the same apple.

7. "Democrats Missed Chance on Iraq, Pelosi Says," Reuters, March 7, 2003.

8. "Summons to War," *New York Times,* August 28, 2002.

9. Quoted in Charles Krauthammer, "Is This the Way to Decide on Iraq?" *Washington Post,* September 20, 2002.

Crazy Liberal Idea #5: Bush Isn't Protecting You

1. Quoted in Glenn Blain, "Officers with Kerry in Bronx Irk GOP," *Journal News,* July 17, 2003.

2. David Cole, "National Security State," *Nation,* December 17, 2001.

3. "Unbound by the Rule of Law," a report by the Lawyers Committee for Human Rights.

4. Jonathan Chait, "The 9/10 President," *New Republic,* March 10, 2003.

5. "Gross Domestic Purchases Prices and Related Measures," Bureau of Economic Analysis, www.bea.gov/briefrm/tables/pricedat.htm.

6. Steve Kroft, "Unsafe Ports," *60 Minutes,* March 24, 2002.

7. Gary Hart, "Business as Usual for Chemical Plants," *Washington Post,* August 11, 2003.

8. The hidden purpose of Chait's piece is not to argue for homeland security, but rather to criticize Bush for supporting tax cuts, to which Chait himself is obsessively opposed: "No one should have expected him to transform himself into a New Democrat on September 12, 2001. But he could have scaled back part of his tax cut to make room for the homeland security increase that experts and members of both parties in Congress agreed was needed. . . ."

9. Blain, *Journal News.*

10. Paul Krugman, "Red Blue Terror Alert," *New York Times,* April 1, 2003.

11. Heather Mac Donald, "Straight Talk on Homeland Security," *City Journal,* summer 2003.

12. Jonah Goldberg, "The Patriot Act: Separating Hysteria from Fact," Tribune Media Services, September 19, 2003. See also Knight Ridder News Service, "Memo Shows US Has Not Used Patriot Act to Seek Library Data," September 18, 2003.

6. America, the Good Samaritan

1. Through a strange concatenation of circumstances, Bush's AIDS initiative has been overshadowed at every turn by the war in Iraq. It was unveiled during the 2003 State of the Union address, delivered at the end of January. And it would have been the biggest news to emerge from that speech, and indeed been the dominant news story of the month of February, had the looming war not taken precedence. Bush made his important Good Samaritan speech just one day before he helped pilot his own plane to the USS *Abraham Lincoln*

and declared an end to major combat in Iraq. And when, in July 2003, he took an unprecedented trip to Africa to highlight the AIDS initiative, the press chose to obsess instead over the questionable inclusion in the State of the Union address seven months earlier of an allegation that Saddam Hussein had sought nuclear material in Niger. (See Crazy Liberal Idea #8: Bush Is a Liar.)

2. Botswana, Ivory Coast, Ethiopia, Guyana, Haiti, Kenya, Mozambique, Namibia, Nigeria, Rwanda, South Africa, Tanzania, Uganda, and Zambia.

3. *The News Hour with Jim Lehrer,* PBS, February 16, 2000.

4. Michelangelo Signorile, "The Most Dangerous President Ever," *Advocate.com,* July 1, 2003.

5. John Donnelly, "AIDS Fund Falters as U.S. Plans Grants," *Boston Globe,* January 31, 2003.

6. Bill Sammon, "Bush Praised for Efforts to Help Blacks in Africa," *Washington Times,* July 7, 2003.

7. David Grann, "The Price of Power," *New York Times Magazine,* May 11, 2003.

Crazy Liberal Idea #6: Bush Wants to
Bankrupt the Government

1. Andrew Sullivan, "Hey Big Spender," *Time,* September 5, 2003.

2. Quoted in Jonathan Rauch, "The Accidental Radical," *National Journal,* July 25, 2003.

3. Ramesh Ponnuru, "Swallowed by Leviathan," *National Review,* September 29, 2003.

4. Rush Limbaugh, *The Rush Limbaugh Program,* September 3, 2003.

5. Quoted in Fred Barnes, "Big-Government Conservatism," *Wall Street Journal,* August 18, 2003.

6. Paul Starr, "The Bush Bankruptcy Plan," *American Prospect,* June 1, 2003.

7. Note the use of the term "initiatives," which is just code for "massive new government programs."

8. Arthur I. Blaustein, "Leave No Millionaire Behind," *Mother Jones,* July 21, 2003.

9. Address by Bill Moyers to the "Take Back America" Conference, Washington, DC, June 9, 2003.

10. Unpublished September 2002 statistics from the Internal Revenue Service featuring these data are available at www.rushlimbaugh.com/home/menu/irsfigures.member.html.

11. Robert Kuttner, "State Starvation," *Boston Globe,* April 30, 2003. I am unaware of any occasion on which Bush "crowed" about spending cuts, since he hasn't made any.

7. Thinking About the Unthinkable

1. Of all the pieces of legislation to which he has committed himself, the only one with which he probably truly disagrees is the McCain-Feingold campaign-finance reform bill—which he signed in the midst of corporate accounting scandals that have nothing to do with campaign finance.

2. I write these words with affection and respect for both men; I helped start the *Weekly Standard* with Kristol and have been a close friend of Kagan's for twenty years.

Crazy Liberal Idea #7: Bush Is a Cowboy

1. Maureen Dowd, "Echo of the Bullhorn," *New York Times,* September 11, 2002.

2. Maureen Dowd, "Lemon Fizzes on the Banks of the Euphrates," *New York Times,* September 18, 2002.

3. Maureen Dowd, "It Couldn't Be Verse," *New York Times,* June 8, 2003.

4. Maureen Dowd, "The Xanax Cowboy," *New York Times,* March 9, 2003.

5. Stanley Hoffman, "America Goes Backward," *New York Review of Books,* June 1, 2003.

6. Thucydides, *The History of the Peloponnesian War,* translated by Benjamin Jowitt (Oxford University Press, 1900), vol. 5, p. 177.

7. "The Bush Doctrine," *New York Times,* September 22, 2002.

8. Tom Barry, "How Things Have Changed," in *Power Trip: U.S. Unilateralism and Global Strategy After September 11,* edited by John Feffer (Seven Stories Press, 2003), p. 36.

9. Fareed Zakaria, "The Arrogant Empire," *Newsweek,* March 3, 2003.

8. The Visionary

1. British Prime Minister Tony Blair's dossier of September 2002 that declared Saddam Hussein had the means to launch biological and chemical weap-

ons at Great Britain in forty-five minutes' time. That statement was echoed once, and only once, by Bush officials, and was never uttered again. Bush did not believe that the United States was vulnerable to an Iraqi military strike. Following a months-long parliamentary investigation, the Blair government was cleared of the charge that it had "sexed up" its dossier, because it had been the dominant view of its intelligence officials that indeed Iraq could load WMD in three-quarters of an hour onto missiles that could reach Britain.

2. In this way America was much like Israel, which is never so popular as when Jewish children are being killed and never so unpopular as when it acts to prevent the deaths of Jewish children.

3. "George W. Bush: Running On His Faith," U.S. News Online, undated.

4. The centrality of militant Islam to the problems of the future helps explain why the administration has been able to remain relatively calm when it comes to the nuclear challenge posed by North Korea. It's an evil and crazy regime, but it poses a different kind of threat.

5. The glaring exception to the refreshing clarity, honesty, and beauty of George W. Bush's views on freedom and unfreedom comes in relation to the Saudis. One of the root causes of the war on terror is this fertile breeding ground for militant Islam. We know that fifteen of the nineteen September 11 hijackers were Saudi citizens, and that Osama Bin Laden's fortune derives from his family business there. The Saudi royal family, which numbers more than five thousand, is the funding spigot for anti-Western mayhem. They oppress their fellow citizens, they have spent billions trying to eradicate the state of Israel, and for more than forty years they have funded terrorists who target Westerners and Israelis alike. And, perhaps most tellingly, they are responsible for the dissemination and mainstreaming of the peculiar brand of extremist Islamic religious practice called Wahhabism throughout the world. We know that the Saudi government actively impeded the FBI's investigation into the 1996 bombing of the Khobar Towers, in which nineteen American servicemen were killed. We know that in the days after September 11, the Saudis spirited hundreds of Bin Laden relations out of the United States. And yet George W. Bush, like presidents before him dating back to Franklin Delano Roosevelt, continues to grant the Saudis a peculiarly special status. On April 25, 2002, Bush welcomed Crown Prince Abdullah—the nation's dictator in all but name—to the White House and saluted "the strong relationship between Saudi Arabia and the United States of America."

He continued on in distressing fashion: "Our partnership is important to both our nations. And it is important to the cause of peace and stability in the Middle East and the world. We discussed the critical importance of the war on terror."

Now, it may well be that we are receiving special and dramatic assistance from the Saudi government in the war on terror that neither they nor the U.S. government can make public. That's certainly the impression American officials like to give when they are challenged on the matter of the hypocrisy of preaching democracy everywhere but in Saudi Arabia. But the war on terror will not be won, and George Bush's vision will not be fulfilled, until he and the U.S. government are prepared to confront the nation of Saudi Arabia with its responsibility for the evildoing.

Crazy Liberal Idea #8: Bush Is a Liar

1. Jimmy Breslin, "The Air Is Thick With Lies," *Newsday,* August 24, 2003.

2. Andrew Greeley, "U.S. Sinking in Iraq Quagmire," *Chicago Sun-Times,* August 29, 2003.

3. Al Gore, address in New York to Moveon.Org, August 7, 2003.

4. Joseph C. Wilson IV, "What I Didn't Find in Africa," *New York Times,* July 6, 2003.

5. Quoted in Joseph Curl, "White House Buttresses Iraq Claim," *Washington Times,* July 19, 2003.

6. John B. Judis and Spencer Ackerman, "The Selling of the Iraq War," *New Republic,* June 30, 2003.

7. Stephen Hayes, "The War Against Bush," *Weekly Standard,* June 30, 2003.

8. *Meet the Press* transcript, December 9, 2001.

9. Quoted in Peter S. Canellos and Bryan Bender, "Questions Grow Over Iraq Links to Al Qaeda," *Boston Globe,* August 3, 2003.

10. Quoted in "Bush Overstated Links to Al Qaeda, Former Officials Say," Associated Press, July 13, 2003.

11. David Corn, "The Other Lies of George Bush," *Nation,* September 25, 2003.

12. Joshua Micah Marshall, "The Post-Modern President," *Washington Monthly,* September 2003.

9. "Our Mission and Our Moment"

1. The National Cathedral Speech of September 14, 2001, the Joint Session of Congress speech on September 20, 2002, the 2002 State of the Union, the June 1, 2002, speech at West Point, the June 24, 2002, speech on Pal-

estinian democracy, and the speech before the United Nations General Assembly on September 12, 2002.

2. Statement by David Kay on the Interim Progress Report on the Activities of the Iraq Survey Group, October 2, 2003. Available at http://www.cia.gov/cia/public_affairs/speeches/2003/david_kay_10022003.html.

3. To take one example of an unfair attack: Richard Gephardt, in a Democratic debate in September 2003, said that almost as many jobs had been lost during the Bush administration as during the administration of Herbert Hoover. Such a comparison is nonsensical and incredibly dishonest. The population of the United States in 2003 is 291 million. The population of the United States in 1930 was 141 million. When 3 million-plus jobs were lost during Hoover's presidency, that represented a vastly greater percentage of Americans employed than is true today—especially considering that only 20 percent of women were in the workforce in 1930 compared to 75 percent today.

Index